DATE DUE

OCT 8 '00			

Demco, Inc. 38-293

ADVANCED GOLF

○ ○ ○ ○ ○ ○ ○ ○ ○ ○ ○ ○ ○ ○ ○ ○ ○ ○ ○ ○

Cary Middlecoff

Edited by Tom Michael
of *The Commercial Appeal*, Memphis

 BURFORD BOOKS

Printed in the United States of America

10 9 8 7 6 5 4 3 2 1

Library of Congress Cataloging-in-Publication Data
Middlecoff, Cary.
    Advanced golf / Cary Middlecoff ; edited by Tom Michael.
        p.   cm.
    Originally published: Englewood Cliffs, NJ ; Prentice-Hall,
1957.
    Includes index.
    ISBN 1-58080-025-4 (pbk.)
    1. Golf.   I. Michael, Tom.   II. Title.
GV965.M44   1999
796.352′3—dc21   98-51039
                                                            CIP

About the Author

SINCE TURNING PROFESSIONAL in April of 1947, Dr. Cary Middlecoff has won more tournaments and more prize money than any other player. Since winning tournaments and prize money are the twin objectives of playing professionals, it may be assumed that Dr. Middlecoff is the best.

He is, moreover, a keen student of the game of golf in all its aspects, with an independent turn of mind that has caused him to examine all the theories of the game —and to reject some of them. Although not a teacher of golf on an individual basis, he has done considerable writing about the game.

Dr. Middlecoff was born January 6, 1921, in the small west Tennessee town of Halls, son of Dr. and Mrs.

Herman Middlecoff. The family moved to Memphis when Cary was still quite young, and he began playing at the Chickasaw Country Club at the age of nine. Later Dr. Herman Middlecoff moved the family membership to the Memphis Country Club and Cary did his playing there. He showed much early promise and by 1940 was easily the best amateur in the state.

After graduating from the University of Mississippi and from the University of Tennessee College of Medicine, Cary went into the Army Dental Corps, where he remained until 1945. He practiced dentistry for a few months in Memphis before setting out on a career as a playing professional golfer, promising to resume dentistry in a year if the golf didn't pan out.

Cary is married to the former Miss Edith Buck of Crittenden County, Arkansas, just across the Mississippi River from Memphis. She makes the tour with her husband and has the reputation as "the walkingest golf wife on the circuit," but she never plays herself. The Middlecoffs make their home in Memphis.

In June of 1949, a little more than two years after turning professional, Cary won at the Medinah Country Club in Chicago, to become the National Open Champion. Since then he has been in the very top rank as a golf player.

Cary Middlecoff's Record

1937

Winner, Tennessee State High School Tournament.

1938

Winner, Memphis Championship. Qualified for National Amateur.

1939

Winner, Memphis Championship.

1940

Winner, Tennessee Championship.

Winner, West Kentucky Open.

Runner-up, Southern Intercollegiate.

Quarter-finals, National Intercollegiate.

Qualified for National Amateur.

1941

Winner, Tennessee Championship.

Winner, West Kentucky Open.

Winner, Southeast Intercollegiate.

Quarter-finals, National Collegiate.

Winner, Medidian, Mississippi, Invitational.

Winner, Galloway and Pine Hills Invitational.

1942

Winner, Tennesse Championship.

1943

Winner, Tennessee Championship.

1945

Low amateur Richmond Open.

Winner, North and South Open, 280, the only amateur to ever win that tournament.

1946

Twelfth, Masters, 292, low amateur.

Quarter-finalist, National Amateur.

1947

Winner, Charlotte Open, play-off with G. Schoux, 277—$2,000.

Tied sixth, Colonial Invitational, 284—$700.

Fifth, Inverness, with Sam Snead, minus 2—$450.

Tied sixth, Denver Open, 284—$750

Tied eighth, Atlanta Open, 287—$400.

Tied seventh, Bing Crosby tournament, 217—$225.

Twenty-second Money Winner, $6,119.96.

1948

Fourth, Texas Open, 271—$800.

Tied sixth, Rio Grande Open, 273—$550.

Sixth, New Orleans Open, 283—$600.

Seventh, St. Petersburg Open, 280—$500.

Winner, Miami Four-Ball, with Jim Ferrier, 1 up—$1,250.

Runner-up, Charlotte Open, 274—$1,400.

Runner-up, Masters, 284—$1,500.

Tied fifth, National Capital Open, 282—$750.

Fifth, Inverness Four-Ball, partnered with Jim Ferrier, minus 5—$450.

Seventh, Motor City Open, 280—$800.

Fifth, World Championship, 137.

Tied third, Denver Open, 274—$990.

Tied third, Utah Open, 277—$990.

Tied second, Tacoma Open; five-way play-off with Ed Oliver, Fred Haas, Jr., Charles Congdon, and Vic Ghezzi; defeated on 19th hole by Ed Oliver. 274—$1,070.

Fifth, Portland Open, 273—$900.

Fourth, Glendale Open, 283—$1,100.

Winner, Hawaiian Open, 274—$2,000.

Seventh money winner—$14,621.25.

1949

Fifth, Bing Crosby Pro-Amateur, with Frank Stranahan, 201—$100.

Tied third, Phoenix Open, 280—$833.33.

Runner-up, Houston Open, 273—$1,400.

Winner, Rio Grande Valley Open, 267—$2,000.

Runner-up, St. Petersburg Open, 276—$1,400.

Winner, Miami Four-Ball, teamed with Jim Ferrier, $1,250.

Tied fourth, Seminole Pro-Amateur, 129, teamed with C. Amory—$550.

Tied third, Seminole Individual, 139—$550.

Winner, Jacksonville Open, 274—$2,000.

Tied third, Cavalier Specialists Invitational, 202—$900.

Tied second, Wilmington Open Invitational, 278—$975.

Winner, Greenbrier Individual, 265—$1,200.

Fifth, Goodall, plus 27—$1,000.

Winner, U. S. Open, 286—$2,000.

Co-winner, Motor City Open, tied with Lloyd Mangrum after 11-hole play-off, 273—$2,250.

Runner-up, Washington Star Open, 274—$1,900.

Winner, Reading Open, 266—$2,600.

Tied third, Dapper Dan Open, 279—$1,275.

Seventh, Inverness Four-Ball, teamed with Jim Ferrier, minus 7—$550.

Runner-up, Western Open, 272—$1,900.

Tied fourth, World Championship, 278—$2,500.

Third, Havana Pro Individual, 275—$700.

Tied third, Kansas City Open, 285—$550.

Second money winner—$24,604.57.

1950

Tied third, Long Beach Open, 274—$900.

Tied third, Tucson Open, 270—$900.

Fourth, Texas Open, 270—$800.

Winner, Houston Open, 277—$2,000.

Tied first, Seminole Pro-Amateur, with C. D. Dillon, 128—$1,250.

Winner, Seminole Pro Individual, 207—$1,500.

Winner, Jacksonville Open, 279—$2,000.

Tied third, Wilmington Open, 283—$900.

Tied seventh, Masters, 292—$405.

Fourth, Western Open, 284—$1,150.

Tied fifth, Colonial Invitational, 283—$850.

Tied fifth, Fort Wayne Open, 279--$900.

Tied tenth, U. S. Open, 292—$225.

Sixth, Goodall, plus 10—$900.

Tied ninth, Motor City Open, 282—$570.

Sixth, Inverness Round Robin, with L. Mangrum, minus 4—$600.

Tied twelfth, World Championship, 287—$1,250.

Fourth, Eastern Open, 283—$1,150.

Winner, St. Louis Open, 270—$2,600.

Tenth, Miami Open, 274—$340.

Semi-finalist, Miami Four-Ball, teamed with Ed Oliver—$400.

Winner, Decatur Open, 132—$500.

Sixth money winner—$18,205.04.

1951

Tied fourth, Los Angeles Open, 288—$1,033.33.

Second, Bing Crosby Tournament, 212—$1,250.

Winner, Lakewood Open, 271—$2,000.

Tied ninth, Phoenix Open, 278—$343.33.

Tied thirteenth, Tucson Open, 276—$195.

Tied eighth, Miami Beach Open, 280—$308.

Tied eleventh, Seminole Invitational, 214—$212.

Tied twelfth, Masters, 293—$356.25.

Winner, Colonial Invitational, 282—$3,000.

Fifth, Palm Beach, plus 15—$1,000.

Tied third, Inverness, teamed with L. Mangrum, plus 3—$825.

Runner-up, Western Open, 271—$1,400.

Tied eleventh, Milwaukee Open, 282—$550.

Tied fourth, St. Paul Open, 269—$1,050.

Winner, All American Open, 274—$2,250.

Seventh, World Championship, 279—$1,800.

Winner, Eastern Open, 279—$2,400.

Winner, St. Louis Open, 269—$2,400.

Winner, Kansas City Open, 278—$2,400.

Tied fourth, North and South Open, 288—$516.67.

Second money winner—$24,075.91.

1952

Tied eleventh, San Diego Open, 286—$206.67.

Third, Palm Springs Pro-Amateur—$483.

Tied first, Palm Springs, 134.

Tied fourth, Phoenix Open, 281—$713.33.

Runner-up, Tucson Open, 276—$1,400.

Winner, El Paso Open, 269—$2,000.

Tied seventh, Houston Open, 287—$550.

Tied twelfth, Baton Rouge Open, 290—$190.

Tied third, St. Petersburg Open, 278—$846.66.

Tied twentieth, Jacksonville Open, 289—$80.

Fifth, Wilmington Open, 278—$700.

Eleventh, Masters, 294—$520.

Runner-up, Goodall Round Robin, 348, plus 55—$2,000.

Sixth, Colonial Open, 287—$900.

Quarter-finals, P.G.A. Championship, 1 up 38 holes.

Winner, Motor City Open, play-off, 274—$2,400.

Third, Inverness, with L. Mangrum, minus 1—$3,166.66.

Winner, St. Paul Open, 266—$2,400.

Tied third, All American Open, 280—$1,733.

Runner-up, World Championship, lost play-off to J. Boros 68-70, 276—$12,500.

Winner, Kansas City Open, won play-off 66-72, 276—$2,400.

Runner-up, Southeastern P.G.A., 283—$400.

Runner-up, Miami Four-Ball, with Skip Alexander, 3 and 1—$1,000.

Second money winner—$30,884.65.

1953

Tied fourth, Bing Crosby Tournament, 210—$533.33.

Fifth, Palm Springs, Pro-Amateur, 204—$450.

Tied third, Tucson Open, 269—$920.

Seventh, Texas Open, 270—$520.

Runner-up, Mexican Open, 270—$1,511.

Winner, Houston Open, won five-way play-off 69, 283—$4,000.

Tied fifth, Azalea Open, 279—$606.66.

Tied third, Tournament of Champions, 285—$1,500.

Winner, Goodall Round Robin, 333, plus 42—$3,000.

Tied second, Colonial Open, 287—$2,500.

Tied ninth, Western Open, 287—$446.67.

Winner, Goodall Round Robin, play-off, 333—$2,400.

Tied tenth, All American Open, 282—$715.

Tied fourth, World Championship, 282—$2,730.

Runner-up, Fort Wayne Open, lost play-off to Art **Wall, Jr.**
70-72, 265—$1,800.

Tied third, National Celebrities, 284—$1,200.

Fifth money winner—$19,446.67.

Member of Ryder Cup Team.

1954

Tied third, San Diego Open, 280—$1,600.

Tied seventh, Thunderbird Open, 273—$350.

Runner-up, Phoenix Open, lost play-off on 19th hole, 272—$1,400.

Runner-up, Houston Open, 279—$3,200.

Tied sixth, Miami Four-Ball, teamed with Skip Alexander, 260—$850.

Tied fourth, Seminole Pro-Individual, 142—$475.

Tied twenty-second, Wilmington Open, 285—$25.

Tied ninth, Masters, 294—$781.25.

Tied fourth, Tournament of Champions, 288—$1,375.

Runner-up, San Francisco Open, 213—$1,000.

Tied eleventh, Ardmore Open, 287—$680.

Fourth, Palm Beach Round Robin, 347, plus 16—$1,250.

Tied ninth, Eastern Open, 288—$665.

Tied tenth, Colonial Open, 288—$950.

Tied eleventh, U. S. Open, 290—$300.

Tied tenth, Insurance City Open, 277—$360.

Winner, Carlings Open, 275—$3,000.

Semi-finalist, P.G.A. Championship.

Tied sixth, All American Open, 283—$1,060.

Tied fifty-fifth, World Championship, 292—$200.

Tied fourth, National Celebrities, 281—$2,000.

Fifth money winner—$17,593.81.

1955

Tied eighth, Los Angeles Open, 282—$787.50.

Winner, Kansas City Open, 269—$2,500.

Runner-up, Crosby Pro-Amateur, 196—$1,000.

Tied forty-first, San Diego Open, 289.

Tied thirtieth, Thunderbird Open, 275—$255.

Tied second, Phoenix Open, 276—$1,600.

Tied fourth, Baton Rouge Open, 279—$750.

Winner, St. Petersburg Open, 274—$2,200.

Tied eighteenth, Miami Beach Open, 279—$160.

Winner, Masters, 279—$5,000.

Tied fifth, Tournament of Champions, 296—$1,236.66.

Tied fourth, Colonial Open, 287—$1,430.

Tied second, Hot Springs Open, 275—$1,600.

Tied eighth, Kansas City Open, 280—$710.

Sixth, Palm Beach Round Robin, 349 even—$850.

Tied twenty-first, National Open, 303—$226.

Winner, Western Open, 272—$2,400.

Winner, Miller Open, 265—$6,000.

Runner-up, P.G.A. Championship—$3,000.

Tied fifteenth, All American Open, 287—$506.66.

Tied sixteenth, World Championship, 289—$650.

Winner, Cavalcade of Golf, 276—$10,000.

Third, Sponsors Open, 278—$2,800.

Second money winner—$39,567.27.

Member of Ryder Cup Team.

1956

Fourth, Los Angeles Open, 277—$1,800.

Winner, Bing Crosby Tournament, 202—$2,500.

Runner-up, Thunderbird Open, 270—$1,000.

Winner, Phoenix Open, 276—$2,400.

Tied eleventh, Baton Rouge Open, 285—$246.

Tied sixth, St. Petersburg Open, 278—$690.

Third, Masters Tournament, 291—$3,700.

Second, Las Vegas Tournament of Champions, 289—$4,000.

Tied first, Texas International, lost play-off, 267—$6,000.

Fourth, Hot Springs Tournament, 276—$900.

Tied seventh, Tam-O-Shanter All American—$912.

Tied ninth, Tam-O-Shanter World Championship—$1,500.

Seventh, Miller High Life Open at Milwaukee—$1,300.

Eighth, Western Open at San Francisco—$420.

Preface

IT IS MY INTENTION in this book to give golfers of all types the benefit of the things I have learned in roughly ten years as a playing professional.

One of the reasons that moved me to write this book was that I saw so many club players who did not take full advantage—or anywhere near full advantage— of the ability they had. And I know very well that the game is at its most enjoyable when played to the best of the player's ability.

I have seen players try to fight the wind by over-swinging and pressing, apparently quite unaware that they were going about the problem exactly backwards. I have seen them leave the ball in sand traps, or send it sailing over the green from a trap, simply because (as far as I could tell) they lacked a simple understanding of how to play from sand. Frequently it was because they were using an improper club.

I have seen players who consistently underclubbed themselves, thereby ruining a fairly good swing by trying to hit the ball harder than it was possible for them to do. I have seen players add strokes to their score through failure to apply any sort of tactics, strategy, or foresight to the play of a golf hole—and often these were men who were as cagey as all get-out in running a business.

I have seen players lose tournament matches they wanted very badly to win—and should have won—simply because they took the wrong attitude about playing golf in competition. Frequently they let one natural mistake convince them their cause was hopeless.

To many hundreds of these I have wanted to offer some friendly advice on the spot. But it was seldom possible or feasible to do this.

Similarly, I have been asked thousands of questions about my own golf when I hadn't the time to give a full explanation, thus very possibly leaving a wrong impression with the questioner. For instance, I have been asked times without number about the weights, lengths, and numbers of the clubs I use. I can answer this question fairly readily, but am seldom able to go into a full discussion of why the clubs I use might not be suitable for the person who is asking the question. In this book I try to give a full answer to that question.

Most especially since the 1956 Bing Crosby Tournament, I have been given credit (and I hope deservedly so) for knowing a great deal about playing golf in wet weather. Many friends have asked for some tips on this problem. The tips are in this book.

No attempt is made in this book to dissect the golf swing. I believe that this kind of thing can be easily overdone, to the detriment of those who read it and try to pattern their swings after that of some player whose swing they have read about. I do not ask the reader to swing the way I do, but only to observe the fundamentals of good golf as I try to do.

Playing golf against the best competition week after week, and being obliged to study the game in order to survive, I feel it is only natural that I would pick up some knowledge of the game not readily available to those who play twice a week or so with friends. And in this book I try to pass along that knowledge.

It is my wish that, after reading this book, you will be a more consistent scorer—and a more consistent winner. I know that I enjoy winning at golf very keenly.

My observation leads me to believe that all golfers do. If this book helps you to win, it will have achieved its purpose.

CARY MIDDLECOFF

Table of Contents

TABLE OF CONTENTS

1

Hitting the Ball

ANY TRULY SOUND golf game, to my way of thinking, must be based on the principle of simplicity. The more complicated the swing, the less consistent game it will produce, and the more likely it will be to break down during crucial moments.

I like to think of the backswing simply as a means of getting the hands in the proper position to deliver the hit, and of the downswing simply as a means of bringing the clubhead into the ball square to the line of flight. And I like to think of both the backswing and the downswing as component parts of a single unit.

I am well aware that there are many, many little things that can throw a golf swing out of kilter. But my firm belief, based on years of experience, is that to try to think of all these things at once while hitting a golf ball is to make good golf—or even fair golf—quite impossible.

The basic idea in putting together a golf swing is to get one that varies as little as possible from shot to shot, one that can be depended on to produce the same or similar results time after time.

Step "A" in acquiring such a swing is to get a sound grip. The grip is clearly basic in golf because it provides the only contact between the club and the swinger—you. The grip largely determines how your hands will function during the swing, and the way your hands function absolutely determines where the ball will go on the shot.

In my view, all the other phases of the golf swing are secondary to the function of the hands. The body movements on the backswing are made for the purpose of getting the hands into the proper position and working in the proper tempo. The movements of the downswing can be said to be for the purpose of getting the

2

body out of the way so that the hands can follow the proper course. If a certain hip movement, for instance, causes a slice, it is because that movement makes the hands bring the clubhead into the ball on a wrong line.

The happy part about this is that, given the opportunity, the hands will nearly always do just about as they should. We do so many things with the hands in the natural course of living that they are exceedingly well trained.

Since no two persons have hands exactly alike, it is patently impossible to prescribe a single grip that will be suitable for everybody. But the grips used by the leading players over the years have many points in common, so that we can hardly go wrong in adopting a grip basically similar to that used by the majority of the game's best.

With that thought in mind, I will describe my own grip as an example. It differs in small ways from those of other tournament players, but is in no way radical.

The grip with my left hand is a combination palm and finger grip. The V formed by the thumb and first finger points toward my chin. Looking down from the position of address I can see the first knuckle on the left hand, and about half of the second knuckle. I grip with the left hand as firmly as I can without setting up

3

tension in the muscles of the forearm. There is a slight amount of extra pressure in the last three fingers. The thumb is down the shaft, just slightly to the right of center.

My grip with the right hand is almost entirely a finger grip, with the club lying between the second and third finger joints. The V formed by the thumb and first finger forms a straight line with that of the left hand, both pointing toward the chin. The little finger of my right hand overlaps the index finger of the left hand. As with the left hand, I grip as firmly as I can without setting up tension in the forearm muscles.

This is the grip that I find to be best for me. It permits my hands to work together as a unit, enables me to keep a firm grip throughout the swing, and gives each hand the relative strength it needs for the hit.

I believe that, basically, this grip will be a good one for nearly all golfers. But there is this point to remember: I play and/or practice golf about three hundred days in the year, and the days I do not play or practice I exercise my hands for a few minutes with a gripping device. Thus I keep my left hand pretty strong, almost certainly somewhat stronger than that of the average golfer. For this reason it may be wiser for most players to place the left hand in a little stronger position than I do. That simply means placing it so that in looking down from the address position you can see the first two knuckles on the hand, or perhaps two and a half knuckles. That is in contrast to my seeing a knuckle and a half.

This change also would be reflected in the V formed by the thumb and first finger, instead of pointing to the chin as mine does, pointing about toward the right shoulder. In the grip most favored some years ago, the player was advised that he should be able to see three knuckles on the left hand, but now nearly all the leading players agree that this position gave the left hand too much relative strength, and tended to induce a rolling of the hands as the club came into the ball. My thought is that two and a half knuckles should be the maximum; one knuckle the minimum.

Once you have found the grip best suited for your own game, you must keep a constant check on it. It is very easy to make small grip changes without being aware of it, and these small changes can reflect big differences in your results.

I can see little or nothing to be gained by arguing the merits of the overlapping grip over the interlocking —in which the little finger of the right hand is linked with the first finger of the left hand, instead of being laid over the top of it. Lloyd Mangrum has played wonderful golf for years using the interlocking grip. It is my belief that he also would have played wonderful golf with the overlapping grip.

One very good player—Bob Rosburg of San Francisco—uses neither the interlocking nor overlapping, preferring what is usually called the two-handed grip, with all the fingers of both hands being on the shaft. I consider this a very strong grip, but I believe it makes control harder to achieve.

There is one other grip that I know of that has been used with great success. Gene Sarazen, whose record certainly speaks for itself, always used a grip in which the left thumb was around the shaft rather than on top of it. Henry Picard also used that type of grip with great success, although he was forced into it through an injury to his left thumb. As I see it, this grip could only be used successfully by a person with small hands.

Going a little further into the placement of the right hand, the more it comes over the top of the shaft the weaker its relative position becomes. In general, it should be placed so that the V formed by its thumb and index finger is in a straight line with the V of the left hand, and you should, by looking down at address, see about half the first knuckle—never more than a knuckle and a half. Whatever your grip variation, the V's of the hands both should point well within the body; that is, never outside the right shoulder in the case of the right hand, and the left shoulder in the case of the left hand. The exception here would be in case you wanted to hit an extreme slice or hook, as is taken up in another chapter.

The second major point in acquiring a sound golf swing is to assume a reasonably erect and comfortable posture at address. I favor a square stance for the wood shots and longer irons, changing to a slightly open stance for the shorter irons and the less-than-full shots. A square stance is one in which the toes of both feet are even with the intended line of flight. In the open stance, the right foot is advanced a bit forward of the line, and tends to restrict body turn. I use the closed stance, in which the right foot is withdrawn a little behind the line, only for deliberate hooks.

As with the grip, I am convinced that no single positioning of the feet is best for all players. Due to anatomical differences and swing characteristics, certain players may benefit from slight variations of stance. Stand on the first tee at any major tournament and you will see many fine players addressing the ball in different stances. You will not, however, see any great differences among the better players. Unless you observed quite closely, you probably would get the impression that nearly all of them used a square stance.

For the drive and other long shots, my feet are about as far apart as my shoulders are wide. For the shorter shots, the gap is narrowed until for the short chips my heels are only an inch or two apart, with the toes always turned slightly outward. In these respects, too, I am in general conformity with the game's leading players, all of whom understand that if the stance is too wide there will be too much restriction of body turn, and if it is too narrow it will provide insufficient balance.

The weight should be distributed just about evenly, with a little extra back through the heels. The reasoning here is that the force of the downswing tends to pull the body forward, causing you to hit the ball slightly in the neck instead of the center of the club face, and this extra weight through the heels to begin with will counteract this forward pull.

The knees at address should be slightly bent, or flexed, and should remain so throughout the swing. Having the knees in a locked position would set up muscular tension, and would be no more suitable for a golfer about to swing than for, say, a runner about to begin a race.

The posterior should protrude slightly as you stand to the ball for a shot. Your position in this respect should resemble that of a man about to sit down on a rather high stool. This position will assist you in keeping the weight back through the heels during the swing, and will serve to give your arms and elbows room to pass as they come through on the downswing.

The back should be generally straight, so as to give you the generally erect posture we spoke of at the beginning. A crouching position is no good for golf.

The position of the head should be such that you are looking directly downward at the ball, with the chin pointing straight down. I would make an exception in this respect for the type of player who has big, heavy shoulders and a relatively short neck. It will be helpful for such players to turn the head at address a bit back to the right so that the left eye is fixed on the ball. This will permit the needed full turn of the shoulders without disturbing the position of the head, which *must* remain constant until the ball is hit.

There should be a reasonable extension of the two arms, along with as much proximity of the elbows as is comfortable. You should feel neither that you are reaching for the ball nor that you are over the top of it. The elbows each should be pointing at your side pockets.

This is the grip and stance. Comes now the matter of the swing. The idea is to achieve timing, tempo, smooth power. The hands should be swung back together into the position from which they can deliver their hardest controlled hit, with a gradual acceleration of clubhead speed that reaches its maximum as the ball is met. The hands should send the clubhead straight past the ball along the intended line of flight for a minimum of about six inches. The force of the swing should carry you through to a natural finish, with the right leg relaxed and the head pulled up into a position where you can watch the flight of the ball. Remember that the force of the swing and your follow-through should bring the head up *after* the ball is hit —*never before.*

As the club is being swung back, the hips and shoulders must turn, the weight must be shifted to the right leg, the left knee must bend inward, and, if it is a full swing, the left heel must come off the ground slightly. In each instance, the action indicated is solely to facilitate getting the hands into the proper position in a smooth over-all action. That brings on some questions:

How much should the hips and shoulders turn? How should the weight be shifted to the right leg, and how much of it? How much should the left knee bend inward? How high should the left heel come off the ground?

The hips and shoulders should turn in whatever amount is necessary to permit your comfortably placing your hands where you want them. Where you want your hands to be is largely an individual matter. Take baseball pitchers. One rears way back and throws with a straight overhand motion. Another throws sidearm with a shorter motion. Still another throws somewhere between sidearm and overhand. If speed is their aim, the pitching hand goes back as far as they feel it can without sacrificing balance and control. So with golf.

The weight is shifted to the right leg gradually and smoothly, and in such amount as will permit a full backswing without loss of balance.

The left knee should bend inward about three inches. This is simply to facilitate a full body turn.

The left heel should come off the ground no more than two inches. This action also is to facilitate the full

11

body turn. Actually, the left heel should come off the ground as little as possible, while still permitting the full body turn. The reasoning here is that the smaller distance the heel comes off the ground the easier it is to replace it on the same spot. It is essential that the heel be replaced exactly. Otherwise the swing is thrown out of kilter, since you will then be swinging from a base other than the one you started with. As you proceed from the driver to the shorter clubs, the distance the heel comes off the ground is lessened. From the seven-iron down, the heel should remain in place. The inward turn of the knee, plus a slight inward turn of the left ankle, will permit all the body turn necessary on these shorter shots.

The length of backswing is, I feel, an individual matter. Mine is relatively short—considerably shorter, for instance, than that of Sam Snead or Ben Hogan. It is a matter of feeling that the hands are in position for a maximum hit. There is a muscular sense that lets us know what the hands are doing and the position they are in when they are out of sight. But the further back they go the harder it becomes to follow them in the mind—which must be done in order to play good golf. My recommendation to beginners would be to try to develop a reasonably short backswing. But those who have been playing for a long time and have developed muscular habits in this respect probably would be wrong in trying to make a radical change.

I am decidedly against trying to teach a player a golf swing by telling him that, for instance, his hips should be doing a certain thing while his feet are doing another thing and that, meanwhile, his wrists should be doing thus and so. I think that the most important thing about a golf swing is that it should have naturalness and spontaneity. It should be the player's own.

This is not meant by any means to say that I believe that a man should just grab up a club and whack at the ball in the first way that occurs to him. Far from it. He should do the things that are basic to hitting a golf ball properly, and he doubtless needs to be told or shown what these things are; but he should do them with understanding, not solely because he has been advised that they are the proper things to do.

A player can be shown the position he should be in at the top of his backswing, the position he should be in when his clubhead meets the ball, and the position in which he should finish the swing. But unless he knows how to reach these positions with the proper

13

timing, he has learned nothing really worthwhile. Would anybody, for instance, try such a method in teaching another person how to throw a ball?

Let's take up the matter of achieving tempo, or timing, in a swing. The first step in this direction is a series of preliminary movements commonly called the waggle. These small movements are for the purpose of getting the muscles mildly in action so as to bring about a smooth start rather than an abrupt and jerky one—to set up a rhythmic pattern for the swing. With me, this preparatory action begins before I step up to the shot. I start thinking *tempo* before taking my stance, and I walk up to the shot on a definite count. I highly recommend this practice.

Numerous gimmicks have been devised for starting the club back away from the ball. Some say push it back with the left hand. Others have said the first movement of the backswing should be made with the hips. I say that the swing as a whole must be a unified action, and that, therefore, there should be no singling out of the particular part of the body that initiates the swing. It should be just that—the start of a swing.

To facilitate this start, I recommend, as virtually all professionals do, a forward movement of the hands and body to begin the swing. This slight forward movement makes it possible for you to start back from the position of address while in slow action, which simply makes for smoothness of operation.

The clubhead should be swept back low along the ground. This is not an end in itself, but is made necessary because you want a wide swinging arc. And you want a wide swinging arc because it takes a wide swinging arc to put your hands in the proper position to deliver a maximum hit. So you do not say to yourself that "I will drag the clubhead back close to the ground," but rather that "I will swing it back in a wide arc so as to properly position my hands."

At the top of my backswing, I pause for about a full count. I find that this slight hesitation helps my timing on the downswing, and enables me to check my aim and position. This practice, however, is rather rare among the leading players, most of whom say it disrupts their timing. I regard it as strictly an individual matter.

But whether or not you pause at the top of the backswing, the action here must be smooth and unhurried. The time for the conscious application of full power is still about two feet away as far as the hands are concerned.

As the downswing begins, the weight is transferred

to the left leg, the left heel is replaced, and the body begins turning back to the left. All this should be a smooth, simultaneous action. About the time the hands come even with the right side pocket of your trousers, the wrists begin to uncock and full power is applied. The clubhead should be square to the ball and should be sent straight through the ball along the intended line of flight. At the finish, the weight should all be over on the left side and the right leg should be completely relaxed. The power of the swing should carry you to a full finish. The finish itself merely serves to show how well you have carried out the swing fundamentals.

Going back to the start of the downswing, this is the place where most golfers err. *The usual trouble is trying to begin the hit too quick.* In doing so, much power and accuracy is lost. If maximum power is turned on from the top of the swing, maximum clubhead speed will be reached before the ball is hit, which means that the clubhead will be slowing down as it comes into the ball, resulting in decreased power. If the hit is begun from the top of the swing, while the weight is still over on the right side, you are apt to be thrown off balance to some extent. The time to apply the power is when both feet are planted firmly on the ground and the body is moving forward to augment the force applied by the hands.

In general, those are the fundamentals of the golf swing. It is manifestly impossible to keep all of them in mind while hitting a golf ball. What must be done, I find, is to keep one thing in mind. On a particular day, I may be concentrating on starting down slowly. Another time I may single out the matter of keeping my head still until the ball is met and away. But always it is a single aspect of the swing that I try to concentrate on—a sort of checkpoint.

One thought that I frequently keep in mind while swinging is that my right elbow should point downward at all times during the swing. I do not regard this as a fundamental of the swing, but rather as something that will aid in making you carry out the swing fundamentals. We have said that the clubhead must be brought into the ball square to the line of flight, which becomes a physical impossibility if the right elbow flies out and up during the swing. Then the clubhead must be brought into the ball from the outside in—the cut-across. If the elbow is kept pointing downward, it will remain reasonably close to the body, as it should, and

17

will permit the inside-out clubhead action that is essential to meeting the ball with the clubhead square to the line of flight.

Summing up, I would say get you as fundamentally sound a swing as you can get. Make it your own swing—do not consciously copy all parts of another player's swing, although it is certainly wise to pick up ideas from others. Take a good, free cut at the ball, trying neither to swing harder than you are capable of swinging nor so easy that you do not get your full distance. Then, as you begin each round, single out some aspect of the swing to concentrate on for that particular day. Not two; just one. Don't get your mind cluttered up with a lot of nonessentials, but don't stand there swinging with your mind a blank.

Here are my Swing Checkpoints:

1. *Take a sound and proper grip.*
2. *Select a stance to fit your own physical characteristics.*
3. *As erect a posture as is comfortably possible.*
4. *Take a head position that remains stationary until after contact with the ball.*
5. *Maintain proper balance throughout the swing.*

6. *Maintain consistently smooth tempo with every club.*
7. *Start downswing slowly.*
8. *Make certain your equipment is right for you. (See Chapter 2.)*

○ ○ 2

Equipment

T*HE EQUIPMENT PROBLEM* besets all golfers. Failure to solve it properly can cost several strokes per round.

There are a number of golfing types who, in my view, cost themselves strokes because the clubs and/or balls they use are not those best suited for their particular games. The first to come to mind is the player who, through sentiment or a false sense of economy, keeps the same set of golf clubs year after year—the set, perhaps, with which he won some important tournament or match a dozen years ago. Or maybe he feels he doesn't play enough, or seriously enough, to warrant the necessary expenditure for a new set.

By taking either of these two attitudes, the player denies himself the benefit of the many and continuing advances made by manufacturers in golf clubs—better balance, wider hitting area, better grips. And even better looks, for hitting a golf ball is actually easier with a club that looks like a good golf club. It is a matter of proven fact that golf clubs are made better each year. Engineering knowledge and much testing are brought to bear to see that new models are superior in some way to the old ones. The competition between manufacturers sees to that.

I am not advocating here that you turn in your old set every time a new model comes out. I get new irons every year, and I use perhaps two to a half dozen different putters every year, but my clubs get a great deal more use in the course of a season than could be the case with the average player, and I like to change putters from time to time to get a sort of fresh approach to the problem of putting.

Another type of player who costs himself strokes through improper solution of the equipment problem is the one who changes clubs so often that he never gets quite used to any particular set. This is the same type, basically, who keeps in his club locker, or at home, two or more sets, and never is quite sure in his mind which set he should be using on a particular day. (He gets an uneasy feeling after one or two missed shots that he should have in his bag the one he hasn't, and vice versa.)

This is the same type, also, who likes to carry two putters in his bag, on the theory that, if he finds himself putting badly with one, he can shift to the other. But the fact that two are handy makes him tend to be unsure which he should be using for any putt. If only one were available, he could give all his concentration to the matter of making the putt, rather than wondering which of two putters he should have in his hand at the moment.

Still another type loses strokes because he has the wrong fourteen clubs in his bag. He is, perhaps, carrying a one-iron and leaving out a four-wood. Or, though this is less frequent, vice versa. It may be that he is carrying only one wedge when he should be carrying two. In some instances, a player should leave his two-iron out of the bag and replace it with a five-wood. In rarer instances, the driver should be left out, in favor of some other club, and a brassie used off the tee. I shall have more to say on these matters a little later in the chapter.

Improper equipment is most costly to those whose clubs are too heavy, or too light, or improperly balanced, or which lie too flat or too upright, or which have grips too big or too little.

These are faults that can best be diagnosed and cured by your professional. But I think I can offer some general advice that will be helpful, if in no other way than by giving you a basis for talking intelligently with your pro on this subject.

Gone, happily, are the days when all clubs were made individually and by hand, making it necessary to spend months, even years, getting one by one a properly balanced set. Modern golf clubs made by reputable manufacturers are made in balanced sets. Each club may not weigh the same as another in the same set, owing to varying lengths and other factors, but they have the same swing-weight—which is merely weight of the head in relation to the rest of the club. Mistakes in this connection are made, but very infrequently. Which means that if you buy a good set of clubs these days you can depend on it that they are just that—a set.

In this connection, I am reminded that some time after the great Bobby Jones quit competitive golf his clubs were placed on a swing-weight scale to see if they were properly balanced. It was found that the eight-iron was the only one that was out of balance with the others. Whereupon Jones recalled that it was the eight-iron that gave him the most trouble during his playing days. That could hardly happen these times.

It follows logically that a small person should use light clubs, a person of medium build and strength should use medium weight clubs, and a big, strong person should use heavy clubs. There are exceptions, but they are rare.

Let me tell you the basis on which I choose my clubs, and I believe you can relate that to your own experience, with profit. I am six feet, two inches tall, and weigh about one hundred eighty when in my best playing condition. My shirt sleeve length is thirty-three inches, indicating shorter arms than most persons my height have, and my hands are rather smaller than those of most men my size.

For these reasons, I choose clubs with shafts about three quarters of an inch longer than standard, with grips just a little smaller than standard. The over-all weight of my clubs is just about average, but I prefer a heavier than ordinary swing-weight (D-6) because through fairly constant practice and play, as my business demands, my hands, and golf muscles generally, are stronger than most. I like my grips to be slightly smaller in circumference because of my small hands (I can wear golf gloves in either small or medium size, which is unusual for a man of my build).

I feel certain that, if my arm length and hand size were in normal conformity with the rest of my body, and if I played, say, about three times a week, standard size clubs, with a medium swing-weight, would be what I needed.

The fourteen clubs I normally carry are a driver, three-wood, one-iron, two-iron, three-iron, four-iron, five-iron, six-iron, seven-iron, eight-iron, nine-iron, pitching wedge, sand wedge, and putter. I carry a four-wood to virtually all tournaments, and at times substitute it for my one-iron. This would be most likely to happen on a course that required a number of long, high carries, and when wind was not an especial problem. The distance I can get with my one-iron and four-wood is about the same, assuming no wind. Into a strong wind, I can get a little more distance, plus considerably more accuracy, with my one-iron. With a following wind, I can get more distance, and about equal accuracy, with my four-wood.

The main reason I generally prefer a one-iron to

a four-wood is that I have the type of golf swing that enables me to get considerable height with my one-iron. For many players, and for nearly all players who do not play and practice regularly, getting height with the one-iron is a difficult feat. Further, a more grooved swing is a requisite for getting better and more consistent results with the one-iron. This is because the hitting area on the one-iron is considerably smaller than on the four-wood. But the big advantage of the one-iron over the four-wood, for those who have the proper swing for it, is that accuracy is more easily achieved with an iron than a wood. This advantage is more pronounced on shots into a strong wind, where a fairly low trajectory is desirable, since the four-wood has about twice the loft of a one-iron (about equal to a three-iron) .

For all but a few players, I am convinced, the four-wood will be a more valuable club to carry than the one-iron. For a few other players, it will be advisable to carry a five-wood and leave out the two-iron. The type of player involved here would be the one who has trouble achieving consistency with his long irons, but who does rather well with his fairway woods. As is the case with the four-wood and the one-iron, the five-wood and the two-iron are designed to provide about equal distance under ordinary conditions. Whether to choose one over the other would be largely a matter of personal preference.

Another equipment problem not always easily solved is whether to take along both a pitching wedge and a sand wedge. I do, as mentioned before; I find the sand wedge, with its heavy flange to make it "bounce" through sand, indispensable on any course where there are sand traps. The pitching wedge, which is deeper and a little heavier than the nine-iron, is invaluable for those shots from grass that require a high trajectory and a quick stop. This is especially true on shots from close lies—the sand wedge would, indeed, be just about as good as the pitching wedge if we could be assured that the ball would always be sitting up nicely in the grass. But that, of course, is a highly unwarranted assumption. If the lie is a close one, the jutting flange of the sand wedge will keep you from getting under the ball the way you must if you are to keep from blading (sort of half-topping) the shot.

The type of course you are playing will always have much bearing on the clubs you select for your day's play. So will the condition of the course—whether it is baked out and hard, or soft and lush. Another strong factor to be considered is the weather of the day in question—windy or still, raining or sunny. These factors all are in addition to your personal golf characteristics.

Let me describe, by way of illustration, an equipment problem faced during the 1956 Masters Tournament by my friend and fellow Memphian, Hillman Robbins, Jr., a truly fine player. I think you will be able to profit by relating his problem to some of your own, even though the problems differ in degree.

Hillman brought with him to the Augusta National Golf Course for the tournament a total of sixteen clubs—a driver, brassie, spoon, four-wood, two-iron, three-iron, four-iron, five-iron, six-iron, seven-iron, eight-iron, nine-iron, pitching wedge, sand wedge, and two putters. He had, of course, to reduce the number to fourteen for actual play, in compliance with the United States Golf Association rules. (I strongly urge, by the way, that all golfers restrict to fourteen the number of clubs used for any particular round of play. This is a rule of golf, and should not be deviated from regardless of the informality of the game you are in. Only for strict practice should you carry more than the allotted number.)

The Augusta National is a testing golf course that requires all types of golf shots to play it well, so carrying the two through nine-iron was simply basic. That is a total of eight clubs. Distance is a big factor, so the driver becomes quite automatic. That makes nine. There are four par-five holes on the Augusta National, plus some very long par-fours, so Hillman wanted at least two more wood clubs. Some delicate chips are almost invariably required, so he wanted the pitching wedge. And of course he had to have a putter. That brings it to the maximum of fourteen.

Hillman decided, without a great deal of trouble, to leave out his brassie, or two-wood, in order to reach the limit. He reasoned that on two of the par-five holes, the 13th and 15th, a brassie would be of doubtful help, since both holes are less than five hundred yards and he could probably reach them in two, if he elected to try, with a driver and a three-wood, at most. And since both holes are closely guarded by water on the front, he figured he would be hardly likely to try to get on in two if brassie distance was required for the second shot. The other two par-fives are in excess of 525 yards, making it reasonable to assume that three shots would be needed to get on anyway.

As it turned out, Hillman chose wisely. But on one shot during the tournament it developed that he needed a weapon he didn't have. That did not mean he had picked the wrong fourteen from among the clubs he had brought. Rather, it pointed up the one weakness in his game at the time—and it shows how important the matter of proper equipment can be, which is what I am here trying to do.

Hillman's dilemma came up after a good drive on the par-five 13th hole. This one, as you may remember, is a sharp dog-leg to the left, guarded for some 230 yards out from the tee by woods on either side of the fairway. The actual distance varies from about 450 yards to nearly 500, depending on how closely you care to hug the left side of the fairway. A famous little stream called Rae's Creek flows parallel and adjacent to the front of the green. Back of the green are sand traps, shrubs, and trees.

Hillman's drive left him with a little more than two hundred yards to go to carry the green. For him, as far as distance was concerned, it was a two-iron shot. But Hillman's single weakness of that time was to hit his long iron shots on a low line. Thus he was afraid that even if he hit the ball good and solid, with plenty of power to reach the objective, the shot might be so low as to catch the forward bank of the ditch and plunk back in.

That would have meant suffering a penalty stroke,

and as the pin was on the front near the ditch, his next shot would have been a most delicate one. So he elected to try with his four-wood, fairly well assuring himself of safe clearance over the ditch, and with a possibility of holding the green if he could hit the shot just a little softer than his normal ones with this club.

Result: The shot was a well-hit one that carried on to the back of the green and scudded into a sloping sand trap. From a downhill lie in the sand, he got just a bit too much of the ball and very nearly sent it into the very ditch he had so carefully avoided on the second shot. The ball hung on the bank short of the water and he was able to play a marvelous chip shot and scramble out a bogey six.

What he needed for this particular second shot was a five-wood—one that he was used to. But in competition like the Masters provides, a five-wood is too specialized a club. The occasion for using one just doesn't come up enough to permit its inclusion among the clubs a strong player like Robbins should carry. He had made several good shots with his two-iron that he could hardly have made with a five-wood, and he was to make others.

The lesson I am trying to get over here is that the problem of carrying the right clubs is an ever-present one. Give some thought to the problems you are apt to face after leaving the first tee. Think them over and try to carry the clubs that will best help you to conquer them.

I have and carry along with me to each tournament three more clubs, not counting extra putters, than I can actually use on any particular day. I survey the situation before starting the round and occasionally make a change. There was, for example, a change I probably should have made just before starting the final round of the 1956 Masters, and I will tell you about that in Chapter 10, when I describe a round as a means of giving some object lessons in playing in the wind, as well as some side lessons.

I would estimate that the most frequent choice to be made on the average golf course would be whether to carry the two-wood or the pitching wedge. Let's pursue the possibilities here, and in doing so I think we will assimilate some of the general knowledge needed in the over-all problem of choosing clubs for a particular round.

Let us say the course is long and the fairways are soft and lush and that you—our temporary guinea pig —are a short but accurate shotmaker. Further, you tend to hit the ball fairly high on all shots, and are seldom in trouble around the greens. You, then, should take the two-wood in preference to the pitching wedge. An alternative might be to take the pitching wedge and leave the sand wedge at the clubhouse, since a pitching wedge is a fairly effective weapon for escaping sand and with your assumed accuracy you will seldom be in the sand, anyway. (Most manufacturers make a combination pitching wedge–sand wedge, but I like a true sand wedge in my bag.)

But if your course is dry and hard, offering very few exceptionally good lies even in the fairway, you are apt to have little need for the two-wood. The reasoning here is that on hard fairways a three-wood will often be a safer and better choice than the two-wood where maximum distance is needed.

Your counterpart, the player who gets plenty of distance but is not always the soul of accuracy, will almost always be well advised to take the pitching wedge, eschewing the two-wood. His chief problem will seldom be reaching the greens, which is the principal function of the two-wood, but achieving a certain amount of adroitness once he is around the greens. In this, the pitching wedge is most important.

In this matter of choosing clubs, virtually every player has a sort of blind spot. We saw that Hillman

Robbins' lay between his two-iron and four-wood, brought on because he could not always be sure of hitting his two-iron high enough. Another player may find, for instance, that he can hit his four-iron considerably farther than he can his five-iron, and that he therefore has a problem on shots just a little too-too far for his five-iron. The best way to clear up this type of problem is practice, but choosing the proper clubs will be a great help.

In general, I would advise against tampering with your clubs, as you are apt to destroy some of the balance by doing so. A chronic hooker, however, can sometimes be helped by having his clubs made a little flatter in lie, and a chronic slicer by having them made a little more upright. This job should be entrusted to a good club repair man.

In recent years there has been some experimentation with clubs several inches longer than standard—up to nearly fifty inches with the woods and to about forty-three inches (standard driver length) with the short irons. Not much has come of it. A longer arc figures to add some distance, but it is quite easy to get the arc so long that it becomes unmanageable. If you are a slow swinger you may possibly benefit from longer clubs, but the benefits are doubtful.

Some years ago one of the name professionals conducted a rather thorough experiment with clubs considerably shorter and heavier than any of the standard models. This also failed to catch on, leading to the conclusion that the standard lengths, having been tried and proven over many years, are best for almost every player.

One of the most frequent mistakes made by the average golfer is in buying balls that are not suitable for his game. Some balls are designed for experts, and are so marked. But these are usually the most popular with the high scorers. These are the more tightly wound balls, and they require a hard and solid hit to get the maximum of efficiency out of them. The less tightly wound balls will provide better distance for a soft hitter. In addition, they are not as easily cut, and hence will be more economical for players who do not consistently hit the ball solid. Your professional's advice should be followed in the matter of choosing the proper ball.

I wear a full-fingered golf glove on my left hand for all shots except putts. I find that a glove helps me get a better grip with my left hand, and saves wear and tear on the hand. Some good players, notably Ben Hogan, never wear a glove, so it is largely a matter of personal preference. But for those who play no more than two or three times a week, I would advise the use of a glove to provide a firmer and more even grip.

Some players prefer rubber-soled golf shoes to those with spikes, but none are to be found among the playing professionals. Rubber-soled shoes can be effective enough in dry weather, but when the course is wet they will slip even more than regular leather-soled shoes. But whether rubber-soled or spiked, good-fitting and comfortable shoes are a must for good golf. This game is tough enough to play at best, and is virtually impossible if you are uncomfortable.

In this connection, it is of great importance that the clothes you wear for golf should be loose and comfortable. Most especially you should choose a shirt that will not bind you in any way about the shoulders, or, if the day is cool or cold, sweaters or jackets that provide plenty of freedom of movement of the arms and shoulders.

Particularly in tournament play, it is important to have along an umbrella and something to wear in case of rain or sudden change in weather. Being prepared for emergencies is just another part of good golf.

○ ○ ○ 3

The Warm Up

*I*T *IS MY CONVICTION,* based both on experience and observation, that it is as important for the golfer to warm up with a few practice shots before starting his round as it is for a baseball pitcher to throw a few pitches before facing the first batter. About thirty shots should be enough. More than that and you may find yourself tiring on the finishing holes.

Basically, this warm up period has three functions: To loosen the muscles, to discover what your swing tendencies are going to be for the particular day, and

37

to check up on your fundamentals. The first few shots should be hit easy with the short irons, working up gradually to the woods, then tapering off with three or four short pitch shots, or chips.

The first, say, ten balls should be hit with the idea in mind of simply loosening up, plus (and this is very important) setting up a rhythm pattern for the day's play. Swing slowly and easily, concentrating on hitting the ball squarely in the middle of the club face each time. Tempo, or timing, is what you are after in this initial phase of the warm up.

Now you come to the middle phase of the session, time to attempt whatever minor corrective measures are indicated as you progress into full shots. (I say "minor corrective measures," because major swing changes should never be attempted just before starting a competitive round. Save that for longer sessions devoted entirely to practice.) If your shots now seem to be assuming a pattern other than the one you are seeking, check your grip and stance and posture (the fundamentals). See that they conform with what has proven successful for you in the past. If your swing tends toward some basic fault that you know about, use this middle section of the warm up to combat it. For example: If most of your bad shots stem from hitting too far behind the ball, set your mind on keeping your head and shoulders high during the swing, with the shoulders level. If your basic fault is the opposite, that is to say you tend to half-top or top your shots, concentrate on driving the clubhead down and through the ball, with the head down and still.

As you swing into the final stages of your warm up, begin thinking more pointedly about the game you are about to play and the problems you are going to face on the golf course. Hit these shots the best you can, with no thought of experimentation or correction. Now you should be trying to determine what your swing tendencies are going to be for the *particular day*. Sometimes, for instance, you will find that, with what feels like your normal swing, you are pushing the ball off line to the right more than usual. So you make a mental note to be more than ordinarily cautious where there is out-of-bounds to the right. Or maybe your hook is more than usually pronounced. So you resolve to give a wider-than-usual berth to serious trouble on the left.

Put it this way: In the first stages of the warm up, you "think swing"; in the final stages you "think golf."

A rather extreme example of just how important

this warm up period can be came on the last day of the Jacksonville, Florida, Open in 1947. I was six shots behind going into the final 18 holes and had little hope of winning when I took to the practice tee early in the afternoon. The first time I took the club back I knew something was wrong—the muscles in my right shoulder were painfully sore.

Then I remembered that, late the afternoon before, my friend Lew Worsham and I had stopped along the road and done some skeet shooting—something neither of us has done since while playing in a tournament. As I continued to hit balls, it became clear that I could take only about a three-quarter swing and that my shots tended to be low and straight but not very long. So I determined just to sort of punch the ball along that day and try to stay close to par. That turned out to be just the style of play that was needed in the strong gusty wind that was blowing, and the happy result was a 69 and first place in the tournament by a margin of three shots.

It seems that everybody was hitting scatter shots in that high wind and finding all sorts of trouble—just as I undoubtedly would have been doing had it not been for what I found out about myself during the warm up period. Not every warm up period will produce such fortunate results, to be sure, but the point is that much can be learned in a short session if the mind is kept actively on the problem at hand.

Injecting another personal note, there are two small additions that I make to this warm up period. You may or may not find them of particular value. Before I take even the first practice swing I spend a minute or two setting my grip so as to get my hands "comfortably on the club." I sort of keep kneading the grip until my hands feel right on the club, never hitting the first ball until I can achieve this feeling. The other addition is that I devote the last three or four practice balls to very short chips. I find that this little tapering off provides a final readjustment to my timing.

Not exactly a part of the warm up period, but a nonetheless necessary adjunct of getting ready for a round of golf, is the practice putting session. Putting is a highly individual matter, and for this reason I would hesitate to try to prescribe any rules here, except this one: Let your practice putting session follow a definite pattern.

Most playing professionals prefer to begin with short putts and work gradually back from the hole to the approach putts. Horton Smith, whom a great many discerning critics call the greatest putter in the history of the game, Bobby Locke notwithstanding, always preferred to start with very short putts he felt absolutely certain he could make.

As for myself, I like to start by hitting three or four putts fifteen feet or so, not at any hole, the purpose being to get the feel of the green. Then I try some short putts at the hole, working gradually back to longer ones, and ending with three or four approach putts of as great a length as any I think I might get on the course.

That is my way. It may easily be that you can set up one that will work better for you. But in any event, follow some definite pattern.

After an effective warm up and a brief session on the practice putting green, you should be able to step on the first tee with some confidence in your ability to produce one of your better games. You will have, at any rate, the satisfying knowledge that you have prepared yourself as well as possible.

There are bound to be times, however, when you will not have the opportunity to warm up properly. You might be late, for instance, or maybe the course is too crowded at the time to permit a warm up. In such event, my advice is that you take about half a dozen practice swings—no more—with two clubs at once or with one of your woods with its head-cover left on. Swing slowly and easily, trying to achieve tempo. Then on your first few shots concentrate hard on meeting the ball squarely on the club face. If the time element forces on you a choice between taking these practice swings and taking a few practice putts, take the practice swings.

∘ ∘ ∘ ∘ 4

Putting

I TAKE UP this mysterious matter of putting in full realization that any theory I advance may produce disagreement. There are certain principles on which *nearly* all good putting is based, but there also are some good putters who defy at least one of these principles.

Take Bobby Locke for example. Here is a man who for years has been considered the finest putter in the world, day in and day out. And there can be no doubt that he has a valid claim to that happy distinction. Yet his putting stroke is a far cry from the one that has always been considered "classic"—a smooth backswing keeping the putter head low along the ground, and a sweeping forward stroke that lets the putter follow through straight toward the hole. Locke hits sharply down on the ball, with almost no follow through.

Horton Smith, on the other hand, always followed the classic pattern described above, and he, too, was a valid claimant to the title of "world's greatest putter." Another putter of almost miraculous effectiveness is Jerry Barber of Los Angeles, whose stroke also is in the classic mold.

Looking back over all the really fine putters I have seen, I can conclude that they had only one thing in common—all of them hit the ball solid. Some were bold putters who hit the back of the cup with nearly every putt they made; some depended for effectiveness on a feathery putting touch that let the ball barely reach the hole, so that the ball could fall in from any of the four sides. Of these two groups, however, far more really good putters fall into the latter than the former, which is only logical. A putt that is travelling with speed sufficient to take the ball, say, three feet past the hole if it misses, must hit the cup just about dead center to stay in, whereas a putt that has just enough speed to reach the center of the hole can go in even though it is as much as an inch and a half off line from the center of the cup.

It can be stated, then, as a principle—subject to argument, but nevertheless basically sound—that it is better to putt with the "dying ball," as the immortal Robert J. Jones, Jr. described it. This dying ball method, besides making it easier for the ball to fall in the hole, has the further advantage of making the next putt easy in the event of a miss.

The purpose of all this preamble is to make it understood that putting is a highly individual matter, and that in advocating certain ways to go about it I am not trying to get any good putters to alter their basic styles. If I were teaching a man to putt who had no previous experience, or a man who was already an admittedly bad putter, I would try to teach him this classic stroke referred to above. But to any player who putts well with what is seemingly a bad putting stroke, I would say emphatically: "stick to it."

I have said that, according to my lengthy and close observations, the only point held in common by all good putters is that they hit the ball solid, meaning that they almost always bring the center of the putter face into contact with the center of the ball. This has to be an infallible rule of good putting because hitting the ball solid is the only way that "touch" can be achieved—touch being the unconscious ability to hit the ball at the desired speed, or momentum. The putter who tends to hit the ball off-center must on some occasions hit it more off-center than on others, and will now and then, by chance, hit it center. Thus he can never be sure of the amount of power he is getting behind the ball, power being a combination of clubhead speed, clubhead weight, and meeting the ball squarely.

The next most nearly infallible rule of good putting is that the stance and posture must be such that the eyes are directly over the ball at address. This makes for greater co-ordination between hands and eyes. If you find your putting game gone suddenly bad, here is probably the most likely place to look for correction. If you are bending too far forward so that the eyes will look straight down at the point beyond the ball, your chances of putting consistently well are slim indeed. The same is true if your stance is so upright that you will look straight down at a point between your feet and the ball, but this fault is not as common as that of bending too far forward. This rule has been defied with success, but of twenty good putters picked at random, I will virtually guarantee that nineteen putt from a position that permits the eyes to look straight down on the ball.

It is only in this connection (the relative position of the eyes and the ball) that I would hand out advice on the type of putter you should use. Some prefer the blade putter; others the mallet-head type. I think this is purely a matter of individual preference. Most playing professionals, including myself, generally use the mallet-head type. But the aforementioned Mr. Locke always used a blade putter, as did Bobby Jones. So a worthwhile conclusion can hardly be drawn as to which type of weapon is the more effective on the green.

Your putter should be chosen, whether blade or mallet-head, so that its head will rest squarely and comfortably on the ground with your eyes directly over the ball. If you are exceptionally tall, you may need an added inch or inch and a half on the shaft so that this will be possible. A short man may use a putter with a shorter than normal shaft, or he may simply choke down a bit on the shaft.

As a putter weight, some theorists hold that a light putter is best for fast greens and a heavy putter best for slow greens. The fact is that most good putters use a medium or heavy putter for all greens. I believe that here again it is simply a matter of individual preference.

Another point held in common by virtually all good putters is a superior ability to "read" greens. That means the ability to tell how far a putt will travel if started at a certain speed; and how much, if any, it will veer to right or left between its starting point and the hole. This "reading ability" is not of great importance to the player who plays the same course, or the same few courses, all the time; he most likely will come to "know" the greens and thus not have to "read" them. But to the player who plays a number of different courses—and especially if these courses are in different sections of the country—an ability to read a green is vital.

Let's take up first the matter of judging the speed of the green. There are a number of factors. Some are obvious: length of grass, thickness of grass, texture of grass, uphill or downhill, wet or dry. One is subtle (sometimes diabolically so): grain. To understand grain on a golf green, one has only to think of grain in a piece of wood. Putting a ball against the grain of a green is analogous to planing a piece of wood against the grain. There is one major difference—the grain of

49

a piece of wood is usually obvious; the grain of a green often is not.

The best method of seeking out grain on a green is to look for "shine." If in looking from your ball toward the hole the green presents a sort of glazed or shiny surface you can know you are putting *with* the grain, and that your ball will roll a good bit more freely and farther than a cursory glance at the surface of the green would indicate. Conversely, if the surface of the green presents a dull appearance, the direction in which you are looking is *against* the green, and the ball must be hit harder than would seem to be the case.

Bent grass greens, of the type generally found in the North and East, are usually very grainy. This will be especially true if there are mountains nearby. (Grass will tend to grow toward the water and away from the mountains.) Bermuda greens, such as are found throughout most of the South, usually will have a more consistent grain. In fact, the most grain to be found in Bermuda greens results from their being cut predominantly in one direction. But whether on Bermuda or Bent, the shine test is effective.

The first consideration in reading a green is to judge the likely speed of the roll. Pay particular attention to the grass in a three-foot radius of the hole. If the grass near the hole is comparatively heavy, it will be generally safe to "go for" the putt. If the grass around the hole is thin, caution should be the watchword. The reasoning here is that the putt should be struck so as to be travelling quite slowly by the time it comes within a three-foot radius of the hole, and unless the green is thin and slick around the cup the ball should stop close enough for an easy following putt. Where the grass is fairly heavy around the cup you can afford to concentrate almost solely on trying to make the putt. But where the green is obviously fast around the cup, you must give a sizable share of your thought to the possibility of having to hole the following putt. Putting against the grain you can afford to be rather bold; putting with it you must use caution.

At this point it may be well to say a word or two about return putts after one has gone by the hole. There is a considerable and natural tendency on the part of many players to be too timid on these return putts, having been somewhat shaken by seeing the first putt run too far past. In nearly every instance, boldness will pay off on these return putts. For one thing, there is usually a good line to be found on these putts. In rolling by the hole, the ball naturally follows the line of least resistance in finding a place to settle, and will generally follow about the same line on the return putt. So look along the line the ball took in rolling past the hole, make a very slight adjustment for the amount the ball missed the hole, and stroke the ball with confidence. Where you are putting with the grain and the ball slides by a few feet, you naturally then will be putting back against the grain, and unless you emphasize this factor in your mind you are quite likely to be too timid and leave the ball short on the return putt.

BREAKING PUTTS

Several factors are involved in the amount that a putt will veer to right or left in its course to the hole. These factors include the contour of the green, the grain, the force with which the ball is hit, the distance the ball must travel to reach the hole, and the texture of the green.

We shall see in Chapter 11 on Wet Weather Play that when water has accumulated on the green a given putt will break less than it appears that it will, from the amount of slope. This is primarily because the ball will have to be struck with greater force to reach the hole with the water braking it along the way, and secondarily because in going *through* the water the ball will hold its line more easily.

The same reasoning applies when the green is slow because of relatively high and thick grass. It is a principle of putting that when the ball must go *through* the grass on its way to the hole the actual break will be slightly less than the apparent break. But when the condition of the green is such that the ball rolls along the top of the grass, the full apparent break must be played.

Most breaks can be seen if a close look is taken, but—and especially where grain is involved—the break sometimes will be hidden. In such a situation, you must rely on what your mind tells you, rather than your eyes. An example probably is needed here, and I will give you the most pleasant (to me) one that I know:

On the final round of the 1949 National Open at the Medinah Country Club in Chicago, I tapped in a two-foot putt for a par four on the 18th hole for a 72-hole total of 286. I then walked over to the side of the green to watch Clayton Heafner, with whom I was playing, putt from about 10 feet for a birdie three that would have given him a 286. Now it happened that I had had just about that same putt in the third round that morning,

*and I knew exactly the problem he faced. The
putt looked for all the world as if it would break
about two inches to the left if hit at the proper
speed to have it drop easily. Actually, however,
the proper way to play it was for a right break of
about an inch. I had played the way I saw it, hit
it the way I thought I wanted to, and missed it
two inches to the right.*

*I knew Heafner to be a fine, cool and resourceful
player—of the type who would hit this putt to the
best of his ability despite the fact that he knew
missing it would cost him perhaps the best chance
of his career to win the National Open. I watched
him examine the line, saw he was somewhat per-
plexed, and wondered how closely he had observed
my putt from almost the same spot that morning.
I don't mind saying, I was just plain scared. But
when he set himself to hit the putt, I saw he was
playing it just as I had that morning—for a slight
break to the left. Now I knew that all I had to
worry about was the possibility of his unintention-
ally pulling the putt and lucking it in, and I was
glad my opponent was the kind of a guy who
could hit a putt the way he wanted to in a clutch
situation.*

He did hit the putt the way he thought he wanted to, and it curled away two inches to the right of the hole—making me, as it turned out—a National Open Champion just two years and two months after turning professional.

The lesson here is that it is of vital importance to be able to read a green correctly, and that it is also important to observe things in the course of the play that may help you later on. Heafner is a good reader of the greens, but that one he misread. Some few players might have seen some little thing that would have led them to a correct solution of the situation, but it was a very tough break to figure.

All the above mentioned factors that are involved in judging the amount of break that a putt will take must be taken into consideration. The relative importance of each factor on a given putt will depend on the particular situation. In nearly all instances, you should decide for yourself. It is permissible within the rules to receive advice from your partner or your caddy, but I find this to be as likely to confuse as to help, generally speaking. For one thing another person can hardly know how hard you are going to hit the putt, which is an important factor in the amount of break to be allowed for.

Perplexing as the problem can be of *how much* break to play, it is often more perplexing when the problem is *whether* to play any break at all or hit the putt straight for the hole. If there is doubt in your mind about whether to play a break, it can sometimes be resolved by looking at the cup itself. If one side can be seen to be lower than another, even slightly, you can depend on it that the ball will break at least a little toward that lower side. That means, assuming that the cup has been cut squarely, that the green slants a little. Sometimes, also, you can see when walking up to a green from the fairway that it slants a little to one side or the other, a factor you may not be able to detect while standing on the green itself.

But suppose, for instance, that you cannot be certain whether or not a slight break is present on a short putt. You decide to play it straight in. Here it will be a good idea to hit the putt rather firmly, remembering that a slow-moving ball will take a slight break where one that is moving fairly briskly will not. Conversely, if you decide to allow for a doubtful break, play the putt to fall into the hole from the front rather than hitting the back of the cup.

To me, one of golf's continuing mysteries is how anybody gauges the amount of power to be applied on a long approach putt. It is a question I have been asked from time to time, usually by players in the throes of three-putting spells. "On long putts," they tell me, "the ball either goes fifteen feet past or stops that far short, and I'm wasting all my strokes on the greens."

I can only answer that getting long approach putts to stop close to the hole is purely a matter of touch, which I have defined as the unconscious ability to hit the ball at the desired speed, or momentum. Perhaps "subconscious" would be the better word.

At any rate, I have become convinced that to be a good approach putter a player must above all have confidence, which can be attained only through practice. He must practice long putts until he feels that he can, without giving the matter conscious thought, automatically gauge the power needed to make the ball cover a given distance on a given green. He must *not* say to himself: "I must guard against being short," or, "I must be sure not to go too far past." There are, to be sure, situations on certain greens where a player would be advised to make certain he leaves the ball in a certain position for a second putt, and would go deliberately past or deliberately leave the ball short for that reason, but this should be done by intent and not from fear.

My thought here is that the proper mental approach to a long putt is, "I'm going to hole this one out by making the ball fall just over the front edge of the cup." The reasoning, as I see it, is that it costs no more to try for perfection. If you have in mind that you want to get a long putt within, say, three feet of the cup, you are apt to fall something short of your aim and get it about four feet away. So if you picture a perfect putt, it may help you get closer to perfection. And in rare instances you will surprise yourself by achieving perfection. An example:

> In the second round of the Masters Tournament, I came to the 13th hole five under par. On this famous par-five hole my second shot with a three-wood hit on the green about pin-high and rolled about eighty feet past the cup, way on the back of this long green. As I looked over the tremendously long putt, I could only think how nice it would be to get it close to the hole for an easy birdie and go six under par. There were several slight undulations between my ball and the cup,

but otherwise it was a level putt with just a small amount of left break.

I decided that the best way to get the ball close was to try as hard as I could to hole it out. When the ball left my putter, I knew I had hit a good putt, and I watched it roll through the little dips in the happy knowledge that it would probably stop no more than a foot or two away, making for an easy birdie. The ball still had about twenty feet to go when I saw and sensed that it might go in. The gallery sensed the same thing when the ball was about fifteen feet short, and a tentative cheer went up. At five feet short, I could see that the ball was rolling at just the right speed and that it was dead in the middle of the cup. And then "plop," an eagle three.

That was about as big a thrill as I have ever got from golf, and several in the big gallery told me it was one of their biggest golf thrills. It put me seven under par, which was the way I finished the round—65. Bobby Jones, host at this fine tournament, was kind enough to describe that round as the best ever played on that world-famous course. And it certainly helped me win the tournament.

None of us are going to hole many eighty-foot putts, but the point I want to make is that the best way to get close is to try to get in. I think that can stand to be repeated: *The best way to get close is to try to get in.*

Throughout this book I make reference to the importance of deciding in advance precisely how you intend to play a shot, and then playing it just that way. No indecision, please.

In no other phase of the game, I am convinced, is this precept as important as it is in putting. It is unfortunately true that it is often very hard to make up your mind just what you think a putt will do, making it very easy to commit the fatal error of stroking a putt with your mind clouded by indecision. The way to look at this problem is that sometimes you will be wrong in your judgment on how to play a putt, but, on the other hand, a lot of times you will be right. So if you follow your best judgment implicitly and stroke the ball confidently along the line you have chosen, you will miss some putts and make some putts. But if you putt with a wishy-washy attitude about the thing, you will never be a decent putter.

No discussion of the mental side of putting could be complete without some reference to the amount of

time a player should take on a given putt, both in lining it up and in addressing it. On the highest championship level of the game we have Jimmy Demaret,
who putts very quickly and very well, and Ben Hogan,
who putts very slowly and very well. These are but two
of several examples I could cite for each category, so I
must conclude that the amount of time a player takes
on a putt must depend on his temperament.

There can be no doubt that a great many makable
putts are missed because the player stood over the ball
too long. To remain largely immobile in a position
such as a putting stance for more than a few seconds
must inevitably cause tensing or cramping of certain
muscles. And it is all but impossible to putt accurately
with tensed or cramped muscles. Yet a careful aiming
and adjustment of stance are necessary adjuncts to
good putting, too.

Similarly, I have seen many players lose putting
effectiveness simply because they studied the line too
long and too cautiously, eventually figuring out ways
to miss the putt instead of ways to make it. Yet there
can be no doubt that a rather close study of the line is
needed if the player is to putt consistently well.

I think the answer lies solely with the temperament of the individual. I can never forget a six-footer

that Hogan holed to throw the 1950 National Open into a three-way tie involving himself, Lloyd Mangrum and George Fazio. Hogan must have stood over the putt for a full minute and a half—long enough to have insured a miss, I think, by anybody but himself—and he drilled it dead into the center of the hole. And he went on to win the playoff. On the other hand, I have seen such players as Demaret, Mangrum, and Julius Boros hole some extremely important putts with the barest minimum of delay, fuss and bother.

My advice to you is that as you do your practice putting you give some thought to the amount of time you take with each putt. Try to determine what is best for you individually, and stick to that pattern at all times.

PUTTING MECHANICS

The putting grip that has become the most popular over the years calls for putting both thumbs straight down the top of the shaft, with the left index finger overlapping the fingers of the right hand. It is sometimes called the reverse overlapping grip, and it has a number of variations, none of which have proven to be appreciatively better than another—except in individual cases.

More important than the way in which the hands are placed in gripping the putter is the amount of pressure applied in the grip. I have observed that a great many players grip the putter too loosely. And some players err on the other side by gripping too firmly, thus setting up a tenseness of muscle that makes accurate putting all but impossible. The putting grip must be delicate, to permit a sensitive touch, but it must also be steady, to keep the putter head from turning. Gently but firmly, is perhaps the best description of the way you should grip your putter. The chief trouble that stems from gripping too loosely is that it sets us a tendency to re-grab the putter during the course of the stroke. The result of this action is nearly always a missed putt. Grip the putter with sufficient firmness at the outset of the putt, and maintain a steady pressure throughout the stroke.

A theory flourished for a time that the ideal putting stroke called for the left hand to predominate in the backswing and the right hand to take care of the hit. The theory may be basically correct, but it has been proven that conscious application of it will lead only to a jerky putting stroke, and a lot of putts yanked to the left of the hole. The best putting stroke is a one-piece affair, a smooth and continuous action with both hands. Such a putting stroke permits you to concentrate on the matter at hand—which is getting the ball in the hole—rather than on the various separate phases of the stroke.

Putting stances vary considerably, but most good putters stand with the feet two to six inches apart with the weight about equally distributed on both feet. I have found that keeping the weight back on the heels throughout the stroke is very important—just as important as it is on the full swing.

The importance of good putting to low-score golf games is too widely recognized to need a great deal of comment from me. On the other hand, it can hardly be overemphasized. So I should like to close out this chapter on putting with an earnest urging that you spend as much time as is conveniently possible on the practice putting green.

Confidence in your golf game is built in a sort of reverse order, from hole to tee. Its foundation is the ability to hole short putts. If you know yourself to be a good short putter, the knowledge will add to your confidence—and hence to your ability—on long putts, since you will be relieved of the fear of three-putting and can go ahead and take the best chance offered to hole the long ones. Similarly, your play around the greens will be bolstered by the fact that you know you can probably hole out in one putt if you get your chip or pitch reasonably close. The same goes for trap play.

As will be noted later on, confidence in your ability around the green is most helpful on long shots into the green. By simple extension, confidence in your short game will be helpful on all your shots, back to and including your tee shots.

Putting practice is pleasant, practically without cost, and extremely profitable in the long run.

○ ○ ○ ○ ○ 5

Around the Green

THE ABILITY consistently to get the ball up close to the hole from the various positions around the green is a valuable golfing asset in three different ways:

1. *It will save you strokes directly. A good chip or putt followed by a one-putt green for a par means the same on the score card as a par made by hitting the green from well out and two-putting.*

2. *The knowledge that you have this ability to*

chip and pitch well will add to your confidence on long shots and enables you to play them better. Further, this knowledge gives you wider range in planning strategy on long shots, because the player with a good short game can more often afford to play safe on a long shot to a well-guarded green, knowing that his chance of getting down in two more shots is not restricted to hitting the green and two-putting.

3. *A good short game is disconcerting and discouraging to the opposition. Few players can long endure with equanimity the prospect of hitting the green in one less shot than you do and not winning the hole. Sooner or later a series of good chips and pitches will take its toll on the opposition's nerves.*

To start this lesson on play around the green, let's take a very simple chip. Assume the ball is ten feet short of the front edge of a level green and the flag is forty feet back on the green. The lie is a good one. Nothing intervenes between the ball and the edge of the green except ten feet of fairway that is a little too rough to make practicable the use of a putter, and there is no problem of having to put spin on the ball in order to have it stop quickly after it hits.

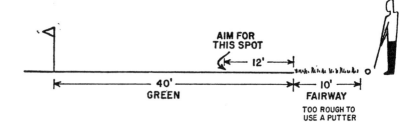

The first order of business is to plan the shot, keeping in mind that it is a simple shot and that you have no wish to make it complicated. Pick out a spot some eight to fifteen feet past the edge of the green where you want the ball to hit. Then pick a club that will give the ball just enough roll from that spot to send it to the hole.

I specify "eight to fifteen feet past the edge of the green" for two reasons: The minimum of eight feet past is a comfortable margin for error and does away with the need for any concern about hitting short of the green in grass longer than that on the green itself, causing the ball to stop short; the maximum of fifteen feet allows you a fairly wide choice in picking a spot that fits in with your own conception of the pattern

68

the shot should follow, yet is still near enough to make for easy aiming.

Let your choice of a club depend on the distance past the front of the green that you have determined that the ball should hit. Your judgment should tell you how much the ball will roll if you hit it with, say, a five-iron, hard enough to carry to a certain spot on the green. It is a matter of touch, in the same way that getting a long approach putt to stop near the hole is a matter of touch. (There are many players who have a "favorite club" for shots of the type described above. I think that is all right as long as these players do not let a slavish devotion to one particular club override good judgment. But I prefer to let the conditions of the shot dictate the choice of the club, rather than vice versa.)

Let's assume now that you have figured out the pattern on the shot and have chosen a club. Say you have chosen a spot about twelve feet past the front of the green for the ball to hit, and have decided that six-iron will give you the twenty-eight feet of roll you will need. Let me emphasize here that this over-all decision as to spot and club should be a firm one; really make up your mind before you step up to the ball.

The stance preferred by virtually all good exponents of the short game is a slightly open one with the heels about three inches apart and the toes turned out. The slightly open stance enables the player to partially face the target, an aid in keeping the ball on line. The club is gripped in the normal way, and choked down about three inches. Stand sufficiently erect to permit full extension of the arms. The hands should be slightly forward of the clubhead; the weight should be, and remain, mostly on the heels.

Swing the club back on a line straight away from the ball. The downswing and follow-through should be straight toward the target. The over-all stroke should be firm and crisp, but also smooth and unhurried. Lest these terms seem contradictory, let me state the proposition from the negative viewpoint: What you must avoid is any change of plan during the stroke —no sudden addition of power during the swing, and no letting up, either. The stroke, you see, should be all of a piece. This will not be difficult if you have made up your mind fully in advance of taking your stance.

It is this sudden change of plan that ruins more of these shots, I am sure, than any other factor. The player reaches the top of his backswing and is seized with a fear that he is going to leave the ball short of the hole. So he tightens his grip and speeds up his downswing, and sends the ball scudding well past the hole. Or he decides his backswing has been too long and that he is about to knock the ball too far. So he makes the fatal error of letting up, which is a major cause of those embarrassing little "poop shots," the ones that go roughly a fifth of the needed distance.

It goes without saying, I think, that the head must remain firmly anchored on these shots. Unless the head remains stationary, there is little hope of striking the ball solidly, and one absolutely necessary adjunct of these shots is that the ball must be struck solidly. In no other way can the player achieve touch.

This shot is properly executed with the hands and arms, and there should be a minimum movement of the body during the swing. Any lateral movement of the body is apt to be particularly disastrous, as it is this type of movement that causes hitting too far behind the ball (the poop shot), or hitting too high up on the ball (blading the shot) —depending on whether the lateral shift is backward or forward. If the shift is properly compensated for, of course, the shot is not apt to be ruined, but the point is that there is no necessity for shifting the weight during the shot in the first place. Body turn on this type of shot will make it harder to keep the ball on line with the target, and is likewise quite unnecessary.

To return to the matter of choosing a club for this shot, I would say in general that the less lofted the club you can safely use the easier the shot becomes. The reasoning here is that the clubs with greater loft will put more spin on the ball, making it harder to judge the amount of roll you will get. If the shot with a considerable amount of spin hits on a spot just slightly softer than you have envisioned, it is apt to stop more quickly than was called for in your shot pattern. Conversely, if it lands on a spot just a little harder than you thought for, you will likely be well past the hole. Moreover, you will have to make this spinning shot travel farther in the air, making it more difficult for you to hit the spot you have picked out for the ball to land on. I think it may be seen, then, that the shorter carry on this type of shot is more desirable because it makes it easier to achieve consistency.

In this connection, however, I would tend to rule out the two-iron and the three-iron, except for shots where the ball is no more than a foot or two off the green, and you wish to play the shot as if it were a putt. This would be the type of shot on which you *would* use a putter, except that you wish to carry over a foot or two of rough ground or heavy grass and on to the green. On this shot, I would not pick a spot for the ball to hit, but would depend entirely on touch, as with an approach putt.

In advocating that you stay away from the deep clubs on this type of shot, I am keeping in mind our premise that there was no problem of stopping the ball. We assumed a level green and the flag well back from the front edge, you will recall.

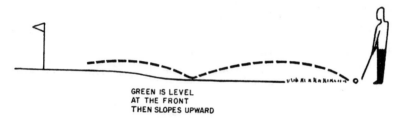

GREEN IS LEVEL
AT THE FRONT
THEN SLOPES UPWARD

With the ball in this same position with reference to a contoured green, the problem may become considerably different. Take, for instance, a situation in which the green is level at the front and then slopes upward and levels out again, with the flag on the upper level. Here we will have a choice of making the ball hit on the level part and run up the slope to the hole, or pitching over the slope with a more lofted club. With the ball no more than ten feet short of the front edge of the green, the run-up shot described above will

73

generally be the safer and better. And on this shot you can add a safety factor by choosing a club that figures to provide sufficient roll if you let the ball hit three or four feet short of the up-slope. Then if you hit the shot a bit harder than planned, it will land on the up-slope, which will cut down on the roll and cause the ball to travel roughly the same distance as it would have, had it hit just short of the slope.

If the flag is positioned well back of this up-slope, it may be the better shot to pitch over it with a more lofted club, especially if the slope is a steep one. But this would be simply a matter of judgment.

If the green between your ball and the flag slants right or left so as to make necessary some allowance for a curving roll, remember that the amount of break you should allow for will depend on the distance you plan to pitch the ball. If you plan to cover most of the distance in the air, you will need to play for only a slight break, but if your shot pattern calls for mostly roll, play a full, or nearly full, break.

Anytime you are hitting this little shot to a green that slopes away from you, it will be best to choose one of your more lofted clubs. The underspin on the shot will be quickly dispelled when the ball hits on a down-slope. Conversely, you can look for the underspin to

74

do its full work when the ball hits on an up-slope. On shots where the green slopes upward from your position and the flag is well back, it will often be helpful to toe the clubhead slightly inward and allow the hands to roll over just a bit as you go through the shot, so as to insure a good roll.

PITCH AND RUN

To illustrate another type of shot, let's move the ball back to about fifty feet short of the front of the green, and place the flag about fifteen feet from the front. On this shot, unless the green is particularly soft

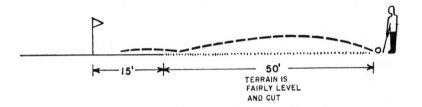

15' — 50'

TERRAIN IS
FAIRLY LEVEL
AND CUT

and holds especially well, it will generally be the wiser choice to let the ball hit in front of the green and roll on. This is assuming, of course, that the terrain between ball and green is fairly level and cut. Here it will be of the utmost importance to make a firm decision in advance as to a definite pattern for the shot. Figure on a certain definite trajectory and pick a definite spot for the ball to land. This is the same advice given on the shot where the ball is to land on the green, but the idea here is to emphasize the point. Any wishy-washy lack of decision on this one can be particularly disastrous, because of the strong temptation it presents to change plan in mid-stroke.

What lends difficulty to this shot—usually called the pitch-and-run—is the fact that it is all but impossible to judge just how the ball will bounce when it hits on even the smoothest of fairways. You can get a good idea about the bounce, to be sure, but seldom an exact one, as you often can on a good green. And the more underspin you put on the ball the less your chance of accurately gauging the bounce and roll. Is the best idea, then, to take a very straight-faced club and try to keep the spin to an absolute minimum? A putter for instance?

No. Because the more times the ball bounces— and it must bounce several times if it travels most of the distance along the ground—the more chances we take. So the main idea must be to hit a happy medium between pitch and run. Take a club that will give you not too much underspin, but which will send the ball over a sizable part of the intervening distance in the air. No exact advice can be handed out here, such as pitch halfway and roll halfway. It is a matter for your individual judgment, based on conditions as you see them. But be sure to pick a spot for the ball to hit where the ground appears uniform and likely to provide the expected bounce. Then concentrate on pitching to that spot.

FROM DEEP GRASS

A few changes in the basic pattern are necessary to getting the ball close to the hole from deep grass. The stance, hand placement, and posture are the same as for simple chip described in the first section of this chapter. But a deeply lofted club should always be chosen for a shot from deeper grass, so as to bring the ball quickly up and out. And the grip should be firmer in the fingers of the right hand, because this shot is essentially a right-hand blow.

The stroke on this shot must be crisp and firm. If there is any looseness as you come into the ball through the deep grass the clubhead may be turned or slowed too much—possibly both. Take a reasonably short backswing, strike a crisp downward blow, and complete the swing with a follow-through toward the hole. If you fear knocking the ball too far, open the face of your club slightly, keeping it slightly open throughout by taking care that the hands do not roll over.

From deep grass behind a bunker, change the pattern slightly by positioning the ball a little nearer the right toe, thus insuring more immediate height. It also may be helpful to open the club face about ten degrees, adding to your chances of quick height. Otherwise the stroke is the same as if no bunker was there.

BUNKER DEEP GRASS

We come now to some short shots that call for rather exceptional techniques, taking up first the shot from directly under a high and steep bank. The stance should be open and the ball should be positioned about even with the left toe—in some instances, where it appears you must knock the ball almost straight up, the position of the ball should be two or three inches ahead of the left toe. Open the club face twenty to thirty degrees. The clubhead should make no strong contact with the ball until it is about halfway under it, and to this end it will be a necessary condition of the shot that you have a lie in which the ball is sitting up at least a little bit in the grass. (A shot from a very close or bare lie will be described later in this chapter.)

Two adjustments will be necessary because of the open club face: Stand as though you were aiming about ten feet to the left of the target, since the open club face will send the ball about that much to the right; and swing slightly harder than you would on a normal shot from that distance, because the open club face will have the effect of making the club more lofted.

Let the clubhead come into the ball a little ahead of the hands, as though to clip the grass out from under the ball. Your follow-through should keep the clubhead low along the ground for about two feet past the ball. (If the bank is closer to your ball than two feet, merely follow-through into the bank.)

Once you have mastered the above technique to a fair degree, you can clear the bank of just about any green or bunker you will find on a normal golf course, provided you have just a fair lie. If you wish to refine the technique a little, practice taking the clubhead back a little outside the line so as to produce a cutting-across action as you come into and through the ball. This will give a little added height and cause the ball to stop a little more quickly.

On a short shot from a pronounced downhill lie,

this cutting-across action will be especially helpful in getting the ball up. But it is next to impossible to get any considerable degree of immediate height from a pronounced downhill lie, even with your most lofted club.

A short shot from an uphill lie, on the other hand, presents little problem from the standpoint of getting the ball up. From such a lie in heavy grass, use a well lofted club to get the ball out. But if the ball is sitting up well on the grass, and with an uphill lie such as you are apt to get when the ball hangs on the bank of a green, choose a club with less loft so as to better gauge distance (an eight-iron instead of a pitching wedge, for example).

THE PUTTER FROM OFF THE GREEN

I think this topic is properly a part of the chapter entitled "Around the Green," rather than the chapter on "Putting," since the operation I am about to describe is basically an approach shot.

Your putter is likely to be your best weapon for getting the ball close to the hole whenever you are no more than about seven or eight feet off the green, and the grass between your ball and the green proper is cut fairly close. The putter also has its uses from farther off the green, which will be discussed below.

An important thing to remember about putts from off the green is that especial care should be taken to strike the ball solidly, catching, as nearly as possible, the middle of the ball on the center of the face of the putter. The idea is to get uniform roll through the higher grass that intervenes between you and the close-cut grass on the green. The putter has a certain amount of loft (about nine degrees), and if the ball is struck too much on its underside it will travel two or three feet in the air before settling down to roll. This will add to the difficulty of judging your distance. What you should be seeking on this shot is to roll the ball along the top of the higher grass. Had you wanted some pitch and some roll on the shot, the wiser choice of club would have been one with which you could pitch the ball on to the green proper—the chip shot.

To get that miniscule amount of loft needed to start the ball off along the top of the grass, position the ball at address about an inch forward of center. The stroke should be, as nearly as you can make it, a sweep, with the ball contracted just as your putter ends its downward arc and begins its upward arc. If your normal putting stroke is such that you tend to hit down on the ball, you should probably avoid using your putter from off the green. (I say "probably avoid" because this business of putting, whether from off the green or on, is a highly individual matter, and I have seen some amazing results obtained with putting strokes I would have to consider unsound. But I am convinced that logic favors the sweeping stroke on all putts, and especially on putts from off the green.)

Naturally, the ground over which the ball must travel on putts from off the green will offer two different speeds of roll. This fact must be taken into account in your over-all judgment of the force you apply to the stroke. But this simply is a matter of touch, which can be learned, so far as I know, only through practice. I would advise that, once you have decided to use your putter from off the green, you concentrate on trying to hole the ball out, as opposed to just thinking in a general way of getting somewhere near the hole. Think of making the ball's final turn take it into the front of the cup.

The putter also is a useful tool on some shots where the ball lies fifteen to twenty feet short of the green, with smooth and closely cut fairway intervening, and the pin very near (fifteen feet or so) the front edge of the green. Here the alternative shot is likely to be a wedge pitch to the front edge of the green with considerable spin. Sometimes, and especially when you have a close lie on the fairway, the shot with the putter will offer the better chance of getting close to the hole. With a close lie, the putter will nearly always offer the safer shot, since even the finest of golfers will at times blade or poop a pitch shot from this type of lie. It was after about two years on the circuit that I discovered that the use of a putter for some shots of the kind described above would save much wear and tear on my nerves. The reasoning here is that a bad putt would likely stop about ten feet past, short or to the side of the hole, making it sometimes necessary to take three shots in all to get down; but a bad wedge pitch might go scudding over the green or go only a few feet from the starting point, leaving a strong possibility of taking four shots to get in.

It should be pointed out that the use of the putter from off the green can be overdone. But if used in moderation and with judgment, the putter can save you many strokes around the green.

o o o o o o 6

Stopping the Ball

CONSIDER NOW a shot from about twenty yards out, under these conditions: The green is guarded by a deep trap that makes it impracticable, if not impossible, to get your ball on the green in any other way than making it land there on the fly; the pin is positioned about fifteen feet from the edge of the green nearest you; and the green slopes slightly away from your side.

A tough situation, surely, and the only way you can get close to the hole is to strike the ball in such a way that it will land on the green and stop quickly after it hits. What I am leading up to, then, is my answer to the often asked question: How do I get backspin on the ball?

The first consideration is to have a deeply lofted club with as pronounced an amount of scoring (grooves, or punch marks) as the United States Golf Association will allow. Here is a layman's definition

GREEN SLOPES
SLIGHTLY

DEEP
TRAP

of that amount: ". . . each groove may not be wider than approximately one thirty-second of an inch, the angle between the flat surface of the clubface and the side of the groove may not be less than 135 degrees, and the distance between grooves may not be less than three times the width of the groove." If the scoring is in punch marks, "the markings must not exceed a slight amount over one-sixteenth of an inch in diameter." Since virtually all modern clubs are made with groove scoring, you may be sure that is the better of the two methods.

It should be added here that another rule of the USGA provides in part: "Clubfaces . . . shall not bear any lines, dots or other markings with sharp or rough edges made for the obvious purpose of putting additional spin on the ball."

All this need hardly concern any golfer unless his clubs are so old and worn (see Chapter 2) that the scoring has begun, so to speak, to lose its grip. The manufacturers see to it that their clubs, especially the deeper ones, take maximum advantage of the USGA specifications.

In this matter of causing the ball to stop quickly, there is one other consideration as regards the club itself: The scoring should be entirely free of all foreign matter—dirt, grass, sand, and the like—when you make the shot. A wooden tee can be used to clean the grooves before the shot.

The maximum underspin (or backspin) on a golf ball is obtained in much the same way as the maximum reverse english on a billard ball is obtained—by a downward blow that first comes in contact with the ball at the lowest practicable point. In this analogy, the scoring on the club face would act in the same way as chalk on a cue tip.

To go back to our shot, and to the original proposition of stopping the ball quickly after it hits, we will find that another factor besides underspin is involved

—loft, or the angle of descent. A pitching wedge or a sand wedge (the pitching wedge is preferable if the lie is a close one in grass, because the bigger flange on the sand club may hinder getting under the ball) will provide the needed loft in nearly all instances. Some extra loft may be obtained by opening the club face and positioning the ball about even with the left toe.

To better understand another important aspect of this hypothetical shot, we have set up, let's assume that the character of the green is such that fifteen feet is just about the minimum amount of roll we can expect even if we make the best shot we can reasonably hope for. Since we postulated that the pin was fifteen feet from our edge of the green, it may be seen that to get very near the hole we must make the ball hit very near our edge of the green, and to get near the hole we must make the ball hit near our edge of the green, and so on. Fall short and the trap has us.

That brings up a number of questions, the combined answers to which will tell us how we should try to play this shot. Suppose we take up first the matter of how high we should try to hit the ball. It follows naturally that the higher the ball goes the farther it must travel to cover a certain distance over the ground, and it likewise follows that the farther the ball is hit the greater the difficulty of making it land in a certain spot. So we must look for a happy medium, one that will best combine accurate placement with height plus underspin. Some further questions that may enter in here are how accurate you normally are on this kind of shot, how great the necessity is for getting down in two shots, the exact character of your lie, and perhaps some others. But these questions are largely mental, and we wish to concern ourselves here largely with the physical aspects of the shot.

So let's assume we have considered all the factors and have decided to attempt a shot that will hit six feet past the front edge of the green, which figures to leave a six-foot, uphill putt coming back, provided, of course, the roll amounts to fifteen feet, as we had calculated. The six feet between the front of the green and the spot we have picked to aim for provides our safety margin, a point that will be taken up momentarily.

Take a slightly open stance with feet close together, a slightly choked grip, a relaxed and fairly erect posture permitting full extension of the arms, and fix your eyes on the ball, which should be positioned a little forward of the left heel. Concentrate on bringing the clubhead into contact with the underside of the ball. The swing characteristics advocated for the chip shot first described in this chapter are applicable here—firmness, crispness, smoothness.

Back now to the matter of our six-foot margin of safety. We know, of course, that if the ball hits no more than six feet short of our intended mark that it will be all to the good. But if it hits an inch more than six feet short, the trap has us, and instead of possibly getting down in two shots (as we hoped for), or getting down in three (our intended maximum), it may now take four shots (which is bad). All of which is by way of trying to emphasize that we must absolutely depend on the safety margin once we have set it up. Had there been doubt that six feet was enough, more should have been taken.

All golf shots from whatever position call for a firm and definite decision in advance as to what, exactly, will be attempted; but on none—unless it be the putt—is this factor as important as on this delicate pitch over intervening trouble where stopping the ball quickly is paramount.

Let's take up now what might be called last-ditch techniques.

For the first one, assume your ball misses the green and stops ten feet to the side of the bank of the green in very heavy grass, and that the pin is placed about fifteen feet from the bank of the green on your side. To make it still tougher, say that the green is a small one and rather fast, and that if you go over it on this shot we have set up, you will be in heavy grass or sand on the other side.

You examine the lie and find that the ball is nestled solidly on the ground in a small depression, making it impossible for your clubhead to get under the ball with a normal shot. You conclude also that the grass is so strong and heavy that a fairly strong stroke will be needed to cut through the grass and get to the ball—a stroke strong enough to knock the ball over the green if it comes out of the grass at all. One more condition: the bank of the green is steep and covered with deep grass, making it impracticable or impossible to get on by knocking the ball into the bank and having it bounce up and over.

This shot is, in short, seemingly impossible of accomplishment through normal methods.

One possibility, however, is left to you: You can take your pitching wedge and deliberately hit about three inches behind the ball, using a full or nearly full swing, just as you would with a buried lie in the sand.

The shot I am advocating that you hit deliberately is the same kind that you must have hit several times accidentally. Have you ever tried a full nine-iron shot, and hit a couple of inches behind the ball? (So have I.) And didn't the ball rise rather slowly and travel about twenty feet in the air? I feel certain this has happened a number of times to any golfer who has played as many as a dozen times.

The shot is, as I have suggested, one you would use only when the situation was desperate. It is, of course, very hard to judge the distance this shot will travel, and in that connection I can only offer this suggestion: You do not hit the ball itself on this shot, but rather you try to take out the divot on which the ball is resting, so you can get some estimate of distance by calculating how far the divot would travel if the ball were not there. I have found that, in general, the ball will travel about twice as far in the air as the divot, provided your clubhead contacts the ground about three inches behind the ball. This depends, of course, on the texture of the ground and on the angle at which your clubhead enters the ground. But I believe it will be helpful in trying to estimate distance on this shot if you think of the ball as being propelled upward as the divot comes out of the ground. A couple of practice strokes before you make this shot will help.

Note that I advise the use of your pitching wedge instead of your sand wedge for this shot. The reason is that the heavier-flanged sand wedge will not enter the ground as easily, and the flange may cause the clubhead to bounce into the ball instead of digging in and taking a sizable divot. If you do not carry a pitching wedge, your nine-iron probably will be more effective for this shot than the sand wedge, because of its sharper leading edge.

Two other possibilities exist for those shots from around the green where a high pitch would normally be indicated, but is out of the question by reason of a too-close lie, a green of such character that stopping the ball on a pitch shot is patently impossible, or perhaps because of overhanging limbs or other obstruction that must be gone under. You can either roll or bounce the ball over the intervening terrain and up the bank, or you can play a "bump shot," in which you deliberately line the ball into the bank of the green with sufficient force to make it pop up into the air and still have enough forward momentum to carry it on to the green.

The possibilities of this bounce and roll shot were forcibly brought home to me on the 77th hole of the 1952 Motor City Open in Detroit. Lloyd Mangrum and I were tied for first place at the end of the regulation 72 holes, and were engaged in a sudden-death playoff, with the championship and top money to go to the winner of the first hole won. We had halved the first four extra holes.

On the fifth extra hole, a par-four, Mangrum's second shot had sailed over the high-banked green and was in the rough about thirty feet from the bank of the green. My second shot was nicely on and I felt assured of a par-four. When I reached the green and saw Mangrum's position, I also felt assured that I was the winner of the hole and the tournament. The flag was on the back of the green. The green sloped downward and away from Mangrum's position, and any pitch shot he hit would have to roll at least thirty feet past the hole. There was heavy grass between his ball and the bank of the green, and a run-up shot looked all but impossible. I well know Mangrum to be a fine, bold and resourceful player, but I couldn't see him—or anybody else—making this shot stop close to the hole.

He did, however, and implicit in the way he went

about doing it is a lesson for all of us. First he looked along the line between his ball and the bank of the green. Then he looked at the bank itself. You could almost see the gears meshing in his brain . . . "If I hit it so hard and so high it will hit here first . . . then it will bounce into the bank . . . and the next bounce could take it just over the top of the bank . . . and it could trickle down fairly close." What happened was that the ball did just what he figured it might do, and stopped about six inches from the cup. We halved the hole. (We also halved the next four holes and called the tournament a tie, splitting first and second prize money.)

The lesson, as I got it, is that almost no shot in golf is impossible provided you have the room to swing at the ball, and that imagination plus the willingness to keep trying as long as even the slimmest chance remains, will often pay handsome dividends.

Notice that Mangrum picked out a possible pattern for the shot, and then stuck to the pattern. He had to have a certain amount of luck, certainly, to get that close to the hole, but the point is that he gave the ball its best possible chance to stop near the cup, thus putting himself in a position to get maximum benefit from the good breaks he got on the bounces. And that's what must be done on this type of shot.

The shot just described was played into a bank that had some slope to it, enabling the ball to bounce forward as well as up, even though the ball hadn't a great deal of momentum when it hit into the bank. Some banks, however, are so nearly perpendicular that a considerable amount of momentum will be required to make the ball "climb" up and over. For this type of shot, your two-, three- or four-iron usually will be best. Position the ball near your right foot, address so as to emphasize the downward character of the blow and thus minimize the chance of having the ball get too much height and clear the bank of the green on the fly.

Pick a spot on the bank of the green for the ball to hit, and simply line the ball at the spot. Ideally, the ball will bounce rather high and be carried a few feet forward by its momentum, stopping after a fairly short roll. But some luck is needed. At times the ball may bounce back despite your wisest choice of a place for it to hit on the bank. At times the bank will be softer than you figured, and the ball will not bounce at all. But as we said, this is a shot to use only when no other reasonable possibilities exist.

95

And as I have sought to emphasize on all these shots around the green, *once you have laid your plan for the shot, stick to it.* It may turn out that your plan will fail because it was not a sound one. But a hesitant, sloppy stroke made because you have not set your mind on some definite pattern, will almost certainly result in failure.

○ ○ ○ ○ ○ ○ ○ 7

The Mental Side
of Golf

PLAYING ANY GOLF SHOT calls for a certain
amount of intelligent thinking; for the exercise of
some judgment; for choosing the best course of action.
If it were otherwise, golf would hardly fascinate as many
people as it does. Ben Hogan, perhaps the foremost ex-
ponent of this phase of the game, calls it "management." That is probably the best word for it; certainly
it is a highly descriptive term.

I would estimate the probable score difference between a player who uses good management on the course and one who does not, assuming other abilities equal, at about six strokes per 18 holes.

This "good management" is not easily defined or described, but I have an idea that all of my readers see examples of it at whatever course they play. I know that at every course where I am familiar with the players, there is at least one who consistently beats seemingly more talented golfers—players who hit the ball farther and apparently better than he does. These "management specialists" manage to win in a number of ways that add up simply to using the head for something other than a perch for a brightly colored golf cap with a tassel on it.

Since there are as many different tactical situations in golf as there are different shots (an incalculable number), no attempt can be made to take up all of them. But a few exercises in some of the problems that often arise on the golf course should provide some understanding of what is needed, from the mental or management standpoint, to cut down our score. Let's take it from tee through green.

TEE SHOT IMPORTANCE

Nearly all golfers have, in varying degree, a tendency to regard the tee shot too lightly. "You drive for fun and putt for money," is the well worn aphorism. Like all aphorisms, this one has an element of truth, but it shouldn't be taken too literally.

The drive, or, more properly, the tee shot, should be thought of as the opening maneuver in your campaign to play the hole well. It might be compared to the first move in a chess game, to the opening lead in a bridge hand, or to the first play a quarterback calls in a series of downs. A good drive opens up the hole to a par or a birdie; a carelessly hit one may put you in a position from which you have to salvage a bogey.

So keep it in mind that the proper place to start bearing down on any hole is right on the tee. Do not wait until you have put yourself in trouble to start thinking.

PLAYING FOR POSITION

The long, straight drive is, for most players, the most satisfying shot in golf. Many golfers, in fact, come very near to considering it an end in itself. They approach the tee with the sole objective of out-driving the rest of the foursome, blithely ignoring the placement of the pin and the location of the most serious trouble on the hole. To such players I seriously recommend a new concept of the term "out-drive." Think of it this way: Your opponent is twenty yards out in front of you, but from his position the pin is tucked behind a gaping trap, and he has left a dangerous shot; you are away, but from your spot the green opens up nicely, and even if your second is a bit short you may still be in position for an easy chip. That being the case, you have "out-driven" him.

Think of the tee shot, then, solely as an effort to place the ball in position for the second shot. Certainly distance is a factor, since nearness to the hole is one of the things that go to make up "good" position. And it is a very important factor. But it is *only* a factor. Keep it in mind that you are playing a golf hole, not taking part in a driving contest for distance only.

To illustrate, let's take a hole that many thousands of golfers know— No. 1 at the Augusta National Golf Course, scene of the Masters. For those who do not know it, the accompanying drawing will make its problems clear.

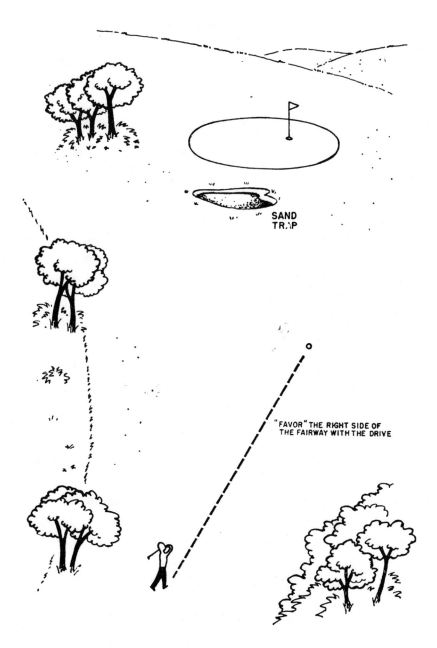

SAND
TR.\P

"FAVOR" THE RIGHT SIDE OF
THE FAIRWAY WITH THE DRIVE

Standing on the tee, we see that the hole measures four hundred yards. It is straight away and presents a fairly simple tee-shot problem, as the first hole of a golf course should. The fairway is relatively wide, and even if the fairway is missed the second shot is not likely to be an impossible one. So we unhesitatingly take out the driver and plan to go for distance.

Before we even tee the ball, however, we check the placement of the pin. We know the green is trapped on the left front, and that there is a fairly wide opening to the center and right of the green. We see that the pin is spotted, say, about twenty feet from the left edge of the green, guarded, so to speak, by the left trap. So we simply "favor" the right side of the fairway with our drive, knowing that if we hit it well our second shot will be over the opening to the green instead over the trap, and that we will have several extra feet in which to stop the ball after it hits on the green. Had the pin been placed on the right side of the green, we would simply have favored the left side of the fairway and achieved the same result. Pin in the center of the green? We would have aimed for the center of the fairway.

That was a pretty simple one to figure. Let's try one that's tougher: the 13th at the Memphis Country

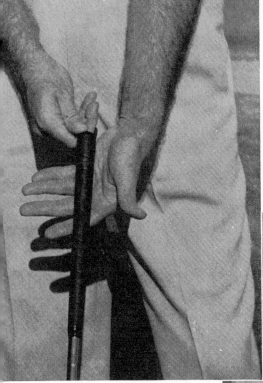

For correct grip, place shaft in left hand in this manner.

GRIP

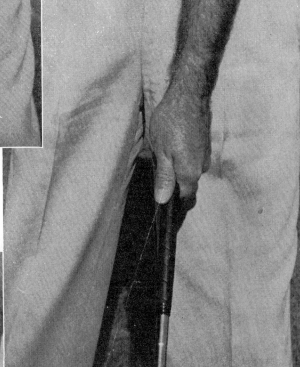

king straight down at left-hand , two knuckles are visible. The mb is down shaft.

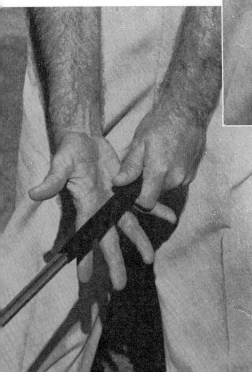

Right-hand grip is more with fingers. Little finger of right hand overlaps index finger of left hand.

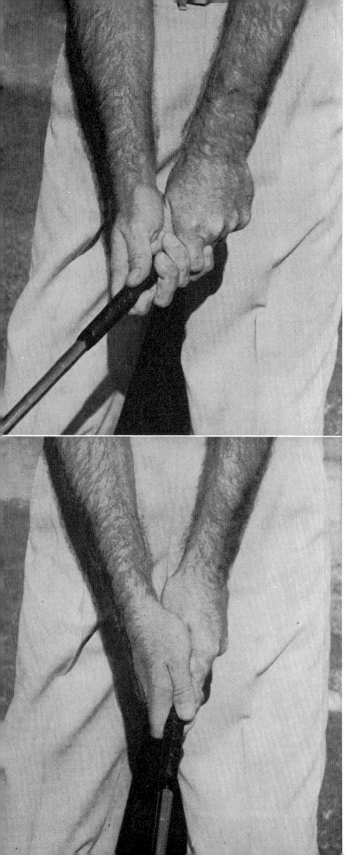

GRIP (Cont.)

Front view shows V of thumb and index finger of left hand pointing to chin, right-hand V pointing to right shoulder, two knuckles on left hand fully visible looking straight down, third knuckle partially visible.

Grip for deliberate slice shows right-hand V pointing to chin. One and a half knuckles of left hand are visible.

GRIP (Cont.)

Hook grip shows right-hand V pointing outside right shoulder. Three and a half knuckles of left hand are visible.

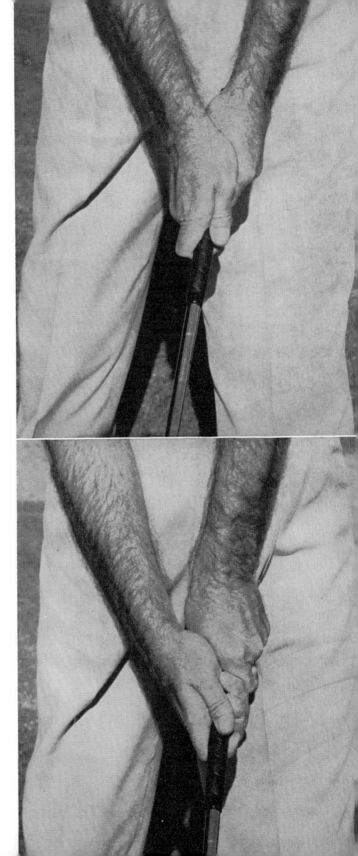

In closed stance, right foot is withdrawn two to four inches from line. I use it only for hitting intentional hooks.

STANCE

In open stance, right foot is advanced from two to four inches in front of line. I use this stance for intentional slices and with short irons.

For the five-iron shot, ball is positioned just forward of center.

STANCE (Cont.)

Stance for fairway wood calls for positioning ball one to two inches inside left heel. This is three-wood stance.

The stance is square, ball positioned even with left heel, knees slightly flexed, eyes on back of ball.

DRIVING

The forward press—a slight over-all forward movement—helps promote a smooth start on the backswing.

The club is SWUNG *back in a wide arc. Weight shifts gradually to right foot. Head remains anchored.*

DRIVING (Cont.)

At the top the weight is practically all on right foot; left heel is about an inch off the ground; left knee and ankle turn slightly inward.

Starting down, the weight is transferred to left foot. The swing continues smooth and unhurried. Note that right elbow points down.

DRIVING (Cont.)

Time now to begin turning on the power. Note that head position remains constant.

The clubhead speed is picking up at this point, as indicated by the fact that it is blurred in the picture.

DRIVING (Cont.)

Still faster and the camera has lost nearly all the club. Note that right elbow is tucked in close.

DRIVING (Cont.)

At the instant of impact, the head is right where it's been all along. Right elbow is still tucked in.

I have hit "through the ball." The clubhead follows after the ball. Right leg is relaxed. Head remains in place.

DRIVING (Cont.)

The momentum of the swing brings me to this position. As the club comes around, the force of the swing pulls the head up.

DRIVING (Cont.)

(LEFT AND OPPOSITE)

These three pictures show that a proper swing permits you to remain on balance. The finish is relaxed and comfortable, just as the starting position was.

DRIVING (Cont.)

Ball is positioned slightly right of center, hands slightly ahead of club-head, eyes on back of ball.

SHORT IRONS

Club is swung back smoothly. Head remains firmly anchored. (The club is an eight-iron.)

At top of swing, left heel is still on ground. Inward turn of left knee and ankle permits all the turn needed for this shot.

SHORT IRONS
(Cont.)

The hands lead the downswing. Note elbow is tucked in close. Left hip turns out of the way.

Down and through the ball—head still in place. Club enters turf an inch in front of where ball was.

SHORT IRONS
(Cont.)

I like to finish this shot with my hands rather high. Note relaxed position of entire right side.

For the long iron, the ball is positioned about four inches inside left heel. Feet are about four inches closer together than for the drive.

LONG IRONS

The club is swung back. The right elbow is tucked in close to the body.

At the top, the right el-
bow points down. The
left heel is about an
inch off the ground.
Nearly all the weight is
on the right leg.

LONG IRONS (Cont.)

Entering the hitting area,
the right elbow is still
in close; the weight has
shifted over to the left
side.

Just before impact, the clubhead is about to be sent down and through the ball.

LONG IRONS (Cont.)

Down and through. The clubhead enters the ground an inch ahead of the ball position. Head still in place.

Two excellent studies of the power position—just before contact (LEFT) and just after contact (BELOW).

POWER POSITION

ck of the left hand is toward the
le. Grip is largely in the fingers.
umb is down the shaft.

PUTTING

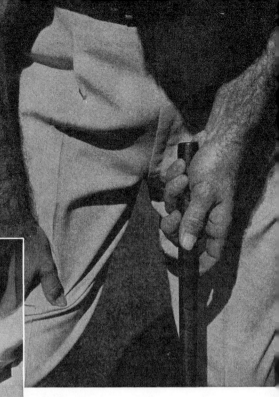

Little finger of right hand interlocks with right index finger. Right thumb also is down the shaft.

his is the front view of my version of e reverse overlapping putting grip.

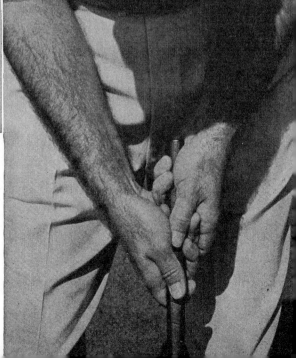

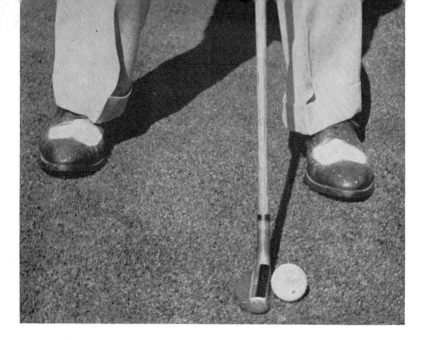

For the straightaway putt, position ball about an inch inside the left heel.

PUTTING (Cont.)

For a putt that breaks to your left, position ball two inches nearer center of feet than for straight putt.

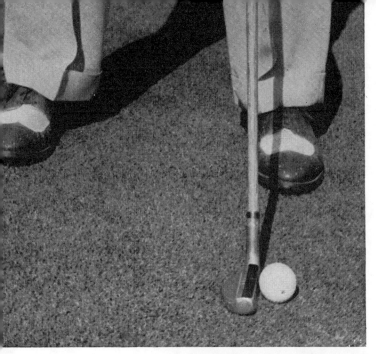

For the right-breaking putt, position ball barely inside left toe. These changes in ball positioning make for better sighting and stroking.

PUTTING (Cont.)

On all putts, hold your position until ball is well on its way. Make this a habit and you will avoid those weak-looking efforts caused by changing position before stroke is completed. Note that head is directly over place where ball was.

(LEFT AND BELOW) Having determined amount you think ball will break on a given putt, aim that far to right or left of hole. Idea is to avoid deliberate pull or push of putt to compensate for break.

PUTTING (Cont.)

Stroke on chip from trap is down and through ball. There should be no intervening bunker. Green should provide rolling room.

SAND

Chip from trap calls for good, clean lie. Weight is principally on left foot, ball positioned near right foot.

The normal clean lie from sand is played with both stance and club face open. The distance the clubhead is shown behind the ball is about the distance behind the ball that it should enter the sand for a shot around the green.

SAND (Cont.)

For the buried lie in the sand, close the club face slightly to get a good digging angle. Again, the stance is open. Clubhead should enter sand a little closer to ball than it is in picture.

roperly hit, the ball will rise very uickly from the sand.

SAND (Cont.)

Stance is open. Dig in with feet for firm posi-tion, club face slightly open.

Club is swung up rather sharply on backswing.

Top of backswing shows restricted arc used on sand shot.

SAND (Cont.)

Starting down, weight shifts over to right leg.

Moving into the ball, the head remains riveted in place.

it under and through
the ball.

SAND (Cont.)

Keep the club face open as the follow-through continues.

but and away, and the hands never completely roll over.

To play from downhill
lie, position ball near
right foot. Idea is to
place ball where bottom
of swinging arc will oc-
cur.

UNEVEN LIES

For uphill lie, move ball
position forward. Weight
should be principally on
right foot to start.

With ball above feet, stand farther away from it. Be sure weight is back on heels.

UNEVEN LIES (Cont.)

_below feet calls for standing closer
t. As in case of ball above feet, get
ght back on heels._

Short shot from downhill lie requiring quick height. Open club face very wide. Bring club across ball from outside in.

To get added height, position ball about even with left instep. Leave club face slightly open.

HIGH SHOT

LOW SHOT

For the deliberately low shot, position ball back near right foot. Close club face just slightly.

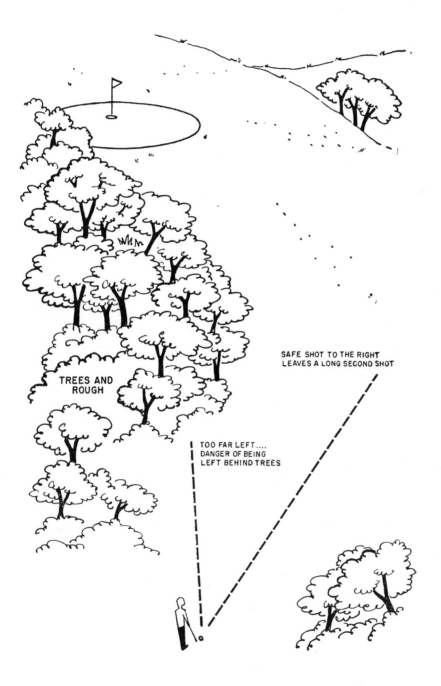

TREES AND
ROUGH

SAFE SHOT TO THE RIGHT
LEAVES A LONG SECOND SHOT

TOO FAR LEFT....
DANGER OF BEING
LEFT BEHIND TREES

Club, scene of the 1948 National Amateur, and a course that presents a wide range of tee-shot problems.

This one is four hundred twenty yards and dog-legs rather sharply to the left. Just about all of our driving know-how can be used to advantage here. The fairway is plenty wide, provided we want to play safely to the right. But the safe shot leaves a long second shot. We can cut off distance by hugging the left side of the fairway, but . . . a little too much to the left will leave us behind tall trees and in rough that is usually left quite high. Score card entries of six and higher come easy if we try to cut it too close to the left and bite off more than we can chew. Par is tough to come by if we favor the right side too much.

First we give some thought to how we are hitting the ball on the particular day in question, and to the tactical situation of the match we are playing. If our tendency is to fade or slice the ball, we may aim down the left side and let the ball drift back on the fairway. A small drift and we have a good drive; a sizable drift and we have a fair drive. If the hook or draw is our tendency, we line up with the right side of the fairway and let the amount of our hook or draw determine the attractiveness of our position.

If we feel we can hit the ball straight away, we simply try to make an intelligent estimate of the amount of distance we can prudently cut off . . . and let fly. (Pin placement is not greatly involved on a hole such as this one; nearness to the green and an open second shot are the prime considerations.)

As may be easily seen, the mental gymnastics I have described here place no great stress on the brain. Neither is any great amount of time required. So for a small effort we can get a sizable return in strokes saved. If you think otherwise, try a round of golf in which you plan a definite pattern for your drives. Make up your mind quickly and positively what you want to try to do. Then take a definite stance, check your grip, and give it your "A" swing. I claim you will save yourself some strokes.

WHEN TO LEAVE THE DRIVER IN THE BAG

This section will be of primary concern to the long hitter, of secondary concern to the medium-length hitter, and of little or no concern to the short hitter. Whether to leave the driver in the bag and sacrifice distance for accuracy involves a relatively simple question: Is the possible reward for added distance worth the risk we must take to get it?

Let's examine the proposition through a specific example—the short but dangerous par-four 15th hole at the Medinah Country Club in Chicago, site of the 1949 National Open.

As we see, the hole is par-four and measures 310 yards. It is mostly downhill, and a solidly hit drive by a long hitter probably would reach the traps guarding the small green. The fairway becomes narrower as it comes nearer the green, and on each side there are dense woods just full of unplayable lies. A long drive would have to be almost perfectly straight to stay in the fairway and remain safely in play. Such a drive would leave us a short wedge pitch, of the type we could convert into a birdie-three, say, two times out of five. But if the drive is off line to any considerable extent, we are threatened with a bogey or worse.

The alternative tee shot is with one of our long irons, or maybe a spoon or four-wood. A well-hit shot with one of these will leave us, probably, a long wedge pitch or maybe a nine-iron. This shot should leave us a putt we can hole about one time out of five. But,

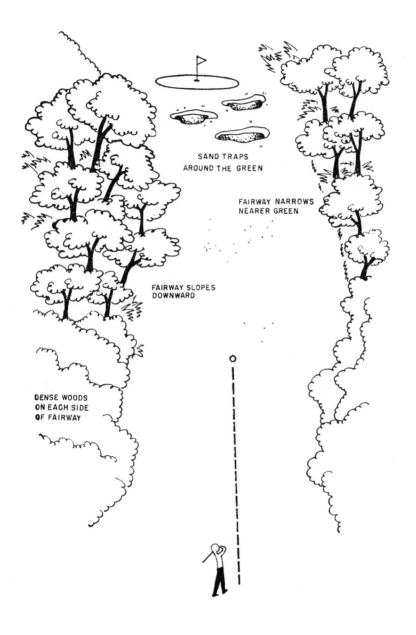

playing it this way, we should be reasonably certain of a par.

So we inquire of ourselves how frequently we hit long drives that are almost perfectly straight. One out of three? That's fair average for a good player. And how often can we hit the fairway (where it is of average width) with a two-iron or spoon? Six out of seven? Probably so.

That's the proposition. Do we need a slide rule to figure the odds? I think not. Just leave that driver in its quiver.

AFTER A BAD TEE SHOT

The exercise of reasonable care in the planning and execution of tee shots will almost inevitably result in an increased percentage of good ones. But, even so, there are bound to be some bad ones. Some will find the rough, some will be bunkered, and some will be so short as to force on us a pattern of play different from the one we had originally set out. Our willingness to accept this new situation for what it is, and to try to meet it positively, will often determine the outcome of a match.

Let's assume we are playing a par-four hole on

which our original thought was to whack out a good tee shot, hit an iron to the green, and have a putt for a birdie. Unfortunately, however, something has gone awry and the tee shot has left us, not one hundred fifty yards from the hole and in the fairway, but two hundred yards away and in the rough. What is needed here, then, is a new plan.

This new plan should be based, generally speaking, on retaining, insofar as is practicable, a good chance for a par and avoiding the threat of a double-bogey or worse. What it will usually amount to is that we must shift our dependence to a good third shot. Back on the tee, remember, the plan was to put the ball in position for a good second shot. It is possible, of course, for even the below-average player to put the ball on the green from two hundred yards out in the rough, but percentages will usually argue against even an above average player staking everything on such a shot.

It will frequently happen that if we choose a club that will provide enough distance we will be taking a risk of leaving the ball in the rough. There is the further consideration that if we try for absolute maximum distance out of the rough, it will be very hard to keep the ball on line. Why not, then, take a club that we can be reasonably certain will bring us safely out of the rough and put us in position for a relatively easy chip or pitch, which, if followed by a good putt, will give us our par?

Keep in mind that if we go for everything on our second shot and it fails to come off, and then the opposition misses the green yet wins the hole with a bogey, we will feel pretty silly. And we should.

Make this a standing rule, in medal or match: Keep the ball in play.

MANAGEMENT OF FAIRWAY WOODS

Intelligent choice and use of fairway woods can save many strokes. Too many golfers, when faced with a fairway wood problem, feel an obligation to take the strongest wood with which they can possibly hope to get the ball airborne, and lash out for as much distance as possible. This type of player is not deterred by heavy trouble around the distant green (trouble that would catch any long shot not hit with absolute accuracy), nor by the threat of the roller that can easily result if a two-wood is chosen when a three-wood or four-wood should be the choice.

No such obligation exists, although in the days of

my youth I must have thought it did. I was many years getting away from the mistaken and often costly idea that a golfer *must* try to reach the green whenever there was even the remotest possibility of doing so. Being a longer hitter than most, and inclined to be proud of it, I looked on all par-fives as "birdie holes." It was not until after I had made many expensive sixes and sevens—and higher—that I came to understand that the first consideration on a tough par-five is to play as nearly as possible for a cinch par, letting the birdies come when they would.

Shorter hitters will have the same problem on many of the long par-fours, as well as on the par-fives.

The point to remember is that the principal objective of a fairway wood shot is to set up the next shot. Often the player should go for the green and try to make that next shot a putt. But the wise player will always give some thought to what the situation is going to be like if the shot is something less than perfect. There is a par-five hole at the Medinah Country Club in Chicago that perfectly illustrates the point I am trying to make here. It is No. 7.

The tee shot on this hole presents no particular problem, except that the straighter the drive is, the better the angle will be for hitting the second shot to-

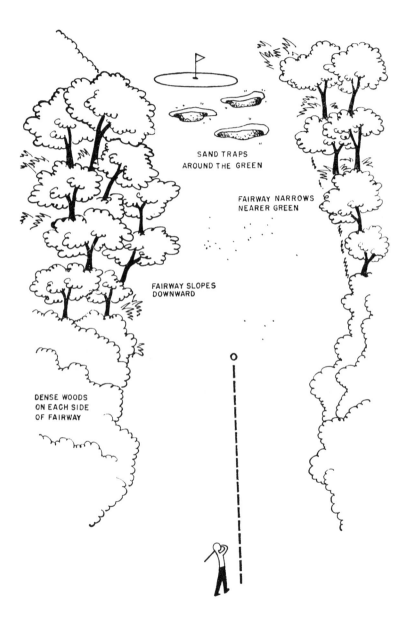

SAND TRAPS
AROUND THE GREEN

FAIRWAY NARROWS
NEARER GREEN

FAIRWAY SLOPES
DOWNWARD

DENSE WOODS
ON EACH SIDE
OF FAIRWAY

ward the green. It is the second shot that calls for thought. The fairway begins to slope downward for the last 200 yards or so of this 475-yard hole, sort of inviting the foolhardy to try to reach the green with a long shot. But as the green is approached, the fairway narrows, and there are woods on each side. Around the green are sand traps.

My experience on this hole during the 1948 National Open will point up the lesson:

It was the last round of the tournament, and I had an exceptionally long and straight drive. I thought I needed to pick up birdie here to have a chance to win. (This was back in the days when I thought all par-fives were put there for me to birdie.) So on my second shot I took a big wood and let go for the green. It was a "good" shot—that is to say it was hit solid and generally straight—but it wasn't a perfect shot, and only a perfect shot would have gone on the green.

My ball stopped just to the left of a sand trap bordering the green, but it was on bare dirt and rather close to a tree. The next one I chipped neatly into the sand trap, where it found a horrible lie up under the overhanging lip of the trap. That meant that I lay three in a much worse position than I would have been in laying two, if only I had used brains on the second shot. I was fortunate to get the ball out of the trap in one blow, and get down in two putts for a six. Good management on the second shot would have had me putting for a birdie-four, with a safe five virtually guaranteed.

That I managed to win this tournament was not due to my brainy play on this hole.

Another opportunity for saving strokes through the exercise of good judgment comes in choosing the particular fairway wood to use when maximum distance is your proper objective. Remember that good, clean lie is needed if the two-wood is to be the right choice. If the ball is settled well down in the grass, pick a three-wood or a four-wood. And on all downhill lies, the two-wood is likely to prove dangerous.

IRON SHOT MANAGEMENT

Using the head on iron shots is largely a matter of picking the proper one for the shot. The general tendency, according to my observation, is to pick the most lofted iron with which the objective can possibly be reached. This is not the proper basis. The idea should be to pick an iron with which the objective can be *comfortably* reached. By so doing, the mind is left free to concentrate on other phases of the shot. This is not meant to suggest that you should take more club than you need, but rather to point out that having enough club in your hands is a considerable aid in making the proper shot. I think you will agree that under-clubbing costs more players shots than over-clubbing does. Remember that you never win a hole simply because you take less club than the opponent does.

Another management problem that presents itself on iron shots is whether to play for the pin or for the green. Here the player must weigh the various factors involved. Is the pin spotted near a difficult trap? Is a long putt from the middle of the green likely to be tricky? How accurate can I normally expect to be with this iron? Am I usually good coming out of traps (just in case)? Is my approach putting normally so bad that I may as well let fly for the pin regardless of the chance involved? What is the tactical situation of the match?

All these factors can be considered in a matter of seconds, and to consider them is to give yourself a better chance for a good score.

Tournament Tactics

IT IS AN UNFORTUNATE FACT that there are many thousands of golfers who are capable of good management and lucid thinking in friendly matches or matches for stakes, but who lose that facility almost altogether in tournament play. This seems to be particularly true in the qualifying rounds of tournaments. "The score card got me," is an explanation I have heard many times from normally good players who have just finished ten or more strokes above their average in a qualifying round.

This type of statement is usually made in an ostensibly humorous vein, but the overtones of genuine sadness can almost always be detected by those who have an ear for such things. In point of fact, it is a sad thing for a golfer who enters a tournament with a light heart and a strong desire to enjoy some competition against players of his own general caliber to find himself knocked out in the qualifying round, simply because he couldn't muster even one of his "fair" games. And something should be done about it.

Just what is to be done may more properly lie in the field of psychology or psychiatry. But since there are so few psychologists-psychiatrists writing about golf (none, in fact, that I know of), perhaps it will not be amiss for a dentist-golfer to hand out some advice on the matter.

The solution, obviously, is to adopt the same attitude for tournament play that gives you your best results in your regular play. And my guess is that your best games in your regular play come when you are keeping your mind on the problem at hand. And my further guess is, if you are the type who plays his worst in qualifying rounds, that in tournament play you let your mind wander ahead to the possible end result of the round. Maybe you ask yourself such questions as

"Won't I feel silly if I don't even qualify for this tournament?" You answer yourself "Yes," and, first thing you know, you don't (qualify) and you do (feel silly).

The thing to do in a qualifying round is go around the golf course concentrating on each hole as it comes, trying to strike a happy medium between boldness and caution. All unnecessary chance-taking is to be avoided in any sort of medal play, especially those chances which may lead to more than a bogey on the hole if they fail to come off. But, on the other hand, a certain amount of boldness is a necessary adjunct to playing a creditable round under any circumstances.

Probably the best mental attitude for any golfer to adopt in tournament play, and particularly in medal play, is that described by Walter Hagen years ago. This great golf tactician said he always assumed at the outset of any round that he would probably make three or four mistakes, and he was thus mentally prepared to take them in his stride. I unhesitatingly recommend this attitude to all players.

When any golfer steps off the first tee in tournament competition he is apt to be more than ordinarily keyed up for the struggle, with a heightened awareness of all golfing situations. With this feeling, it becomes much easier to fall into the error of placing undue emphasis on a missed shot and permitting it to affect subsequent shots. Hence the wisdom of assuming, to start with, that a few shots will not come off as hoped for, and determining in advance to shrug them off and try to make up for them by intelligent application of golfing principles.

Going back to the matter of boldness versus caution, I would advise against any golfer's starting a tournament round with a firmly fixed idea that he is going to play the entire round either with extreme caution or great boldness. He should, rather, start out with the idea that he means to play as intelligently as he can —not "cautious golf," and not "bold golf," but just his "best golf." Then when he is confronted with a situation that calls for a choice between boldness and caution, he can apply the logic that the particular situation calls for. The preconceived notion will simply add to the confusion.

Nearly all golfers who play in only a few tournaments a year prefer match play to medal play. They feel that match play is not as demanding on the nervous system, for the reason that the greatest penalty that a missed shot or mental error can exact in a match, is one hole. And in medal play, of course, a bad shot that puts the player in an impossible situation can cost him the entire round.

To a considerable extent I would agree with this theory, but I would argue that the penalty for a bad or unwise shot in match play can be two holes instead of one, and the thinking in match play should be based on that assumption. The two-hole penalty in match play comes when you lose a hole that you "should" have won. Suppose, for example, that your opponent appears in all logic to be in the process of making a bogey on a hole. You are in excellent position for a relatively simple par. But you take some unwarranted chance that results in a double-bogey and you lose the hole to a bogey. You will then, by any mathematics, be two holes worse off than it seemed you were going to be. Had the match been even, for example, you would leave the green one down instead of the expected one up, and it takes a minimum of two holes to go from one down to one up.

This argument is advanced for the purpose of showing that there is scarcely any more place for too-chancy golf in match play than there is in medal play. The idea in both is to play your own best game, and *to keep the ball in play.*

Take another typical match-play situation: Your

opponent is on the green in two and is thirty feet from the pin. You are in the sand in two and the pin is quite near the front edge of the trap you are in. If you take too much of a chance in trying to get the ball close to the pin, you may leave the ball in the trap and virtually forfeit the hole. What's to do? My experience shows that the first thing to do is get the ball out on the green so you will have some sort of a putt to tie the hole. Do not assume that your opponent is perfect. For one thing, he may three-putt. For another, you may be able to hole your putt for a par—and if you do, that second putt of his is apt to be a lot tougher than if you had floundered around in the trap and made things easy for him.

This business of playing your own game to the best of your ability will prove effective regardless of the type of opposition you are up against. Too many players with little tournament experience fall into the error of deciding before the match begins who is going to win, and playing accordingly. Faced with a match against the favorite in his flight, this type will take all sorts of unwarranted chances on the course, on the theory that he cannot possibly win unless he does something well out of the ordinary. So when some of these chances fail to pan out—as is almost bound to happen

—the net effect is that the match is handed to the favorite on a silver platter.

It is this same type who often is "upset" in tournament play because of carelessness induced by the belief that any opponent he can normally expect to defeat is going to roll over and play dead. Famous last words in tournament golf: "I can beat this guy any time I want to." To which a proper reply might be: "Try it sometime after he has you three down and two to play."

Another common error with many inexperienced tournament players (and some experienced ones) is assuming that the match is decided as soon as a decisive lead is built up on either side. It is my hope that no reader of this book will ever give up in a golf match until he is more holes down than there are holes left to play. It is also my hope that no reader of this book will ever assume he has won a golf match until he is more holes *up* than there are holes left to play.

The history of the game is replete with instances of almost unbelievable comebacks in match play. I once saw a match won on the 19th hole by a player who had been six down with six to play. And I have no doubt that greater leads than this have been overcome.

When a large lead in a golf match is frittered away, it is usually because the player who holds it mistakenly assumes there is no further need for him to work at playing good golf. He thus becomes careless, heartens his trailing opponent by throwing a hole or two to him, and soon the match is even. Then the player who has overcome the lead has the psychological advantage. It is my belief that even more big leads would be overcome, if it were not for the lamentable fact that too many players, finding themselves three or so holes down in the early stages, begin taking unwarranted chances instead of sticking to their own best style of play.

It may be seen, then, that the golfer engaged in match play should not depart from his own best methods either because of a big lead, or a big deficit.

Frequently it has been said and written that the golfer in match play should pay no attention whatever to what his opponent is doing, but should concentrate exclusively on playing against par. This is hardly true. If he has the honor from the tee he should concentrate on making the best tee shot of which he is capable, without regard for what his opponent is apt to do. But if the opponent has the honor and has driven out of bounds, he will hardly want to take even a slight chance of going out of bounds himself, and should definitely aim away from the out-of-bounds line, even if it means taking a chance on going into the rough.

Similarly, if he is away and must play his second shot first and the two tee shots are about equally good, he should play the type of second shot that seems best for him. But if his opponent is trapped or in the heavy rough, he should tend toward a safer type of shot so as to be sure to keep his advantage.

And having two putts to win on the green, he obviously will want to cinch the win by hitting his first putt so it will die near the hole, if it doesn't go in.

But none of these things are in contravention of the basic fact that the golfer in match or medal play should stick to his own best style of play and be swayed neither by current score nor by the reputation—good or bad—of the opponent.

It can hardly be overemphasized that the time to "quit" in golf just never comes as long as the competition is in progress. Many a match has been lost through some small act of misplaced generosity, such as a conceded putt on the part of a player with a commanding lead. Many others have been lost, I am sure, by players who simply quit trying too soon because they figured they were too far behind to hope to catch up.

As to conceded putts in match play, I am of the opinion that no putt should ever be given an opponent, unless it is a foregone conclusion that he will make it. Neither should you ever be miffed it an opponent fails to concede you a putt. Because if he feels there is even the remotest chance for you to miss it, he is entirely within his rights to have you putt it. Sportsmanship here is not a factor. Remember that you are playing in a competition, and you should expect to abide by the rules of the game, which call for holing the ball before going on to the next tee. Your opponent should expect the same thing.

In this connection, if you are about to play a medal round and have been accustomed to playing in games where some putts are conceded, you will do well to practice some very short putts just before starting out. Tapping even a six-inch putt into the hole can be a rather delicate operation if you are at all tense, and unaccustomed to holing the ball on every green. Most of my competitive golf has been played on a medal basis, which calls for holing every putt regardless of length, but I have missed literally dozens of the type of putts that are normally conceded in match play.

The classic example in this conceded putt business occurred many years ago in a PGA match between Bobby Cruickshank and Al Watrous. Cruickshank had a lead of seven up and nine to play and conceded Watrous an eight-foot putt to tie. Watrous eventually won the match. And it may be assumed that thereafter Cruickshank was less generous to his opponents.

A too-conservative attitude on the part of Jack Burke, Jr., enabled me to beat him in the semi-finals of the 1955 PGA Tournament after he had built up a commanding lead on the first 18 holes. He shot a 66 on the morning round of that match at the Meadow-brook Country Club in Detroit, and led me by five holes.

In the afternoon round he appeared to me to be merely trying to make enough pars and get enough halves to let the holes run out on me. With five holes left, I was three down, and I had the distinct feeling that had Burke stayed on the attack as he had in the morning I would have been closed out early.

At the 32nd hole, I made a good birdie putt and was two down and four. We tied the next two in pars and it was then two down and two. The next was a par-five, which I won by getting on in two and two-putting for a birdie. On the 18th, a relatively short par-four, Jack played his second shot to the middle of the green, twenty-five feet from the hole. My second was twelve feet away, and after he lagged up for a par I got mine in for a birdie. I finally won on the fourth extra hole.

But young Mr. Burke got nicely even with me—and with some other people—at the 1956 Masters. He began the final 18 eight strokes behind the leader, Ken Venturi, and four strokes behind me. He shot a wonderful 71 in that terrific wind and picked up nine strokes on Venturi and six on me—or enough to win the tournament.

In the 1952 World Championship tournament in Chicago I shot a 64 in the final round and came from nine strokes behind to a tie for first. In the 1955 Motor City Open at Detroit I picked up eight strokes in one round on Ted Kroll and won the tournament. The game of golf is, in fact, replete with instances that prove beyond doubt that it is never wise to give up. It is trite but true that the game is never over until the last putt is holed.

Playing in the Wind

PLAYING GOOD GOLF in the wind isn't easy.
But, on the other hand, it isn't as hard as a great
many players make it. My view is that most players
need a better general understanding of just how the
wind affects a golf ball in flight. Too many, I believe,
oversimplify the problem by looking on a very low shot
as ideal when playing into the wind, and on a very
high shot as ideal when the wind is following, and letting it go at that.

These two concepts have some basis in logic, but
they fail to take fully into account what experience
has shown me is the most important factor in wind

play—the angle of descent of the ball. Take for example the shot that is hit low into the wind and continues to rise slowly and gradually until the end of the flight, then comes virtually straight down. This shot is often called a "wind-cheater." It is not. It is, in fact, far less of a wind-cheater than the shot that is hit fairly high but levels out during the middle part of its flight, and descends more gradually.

The chief difference in the two types of shots is that the former has more spin on it. And spin is what must be avoided insofar as it is possible when playing in the wind. This is particularly true when the shot is hit into an adverse wind, but it is likewise true of many shots played with a favoring wind. The answer is that the smaller amount of spin makes for better control and, especially on shots hit into the wind, better distance.

Let's take up first the problems attendant upon playing shots into the wind. For nearly all players these are the toughest, except, of course, on short shots where the problem is one of stopping the ball quickly after it hits. On those, naturally, the wind blowing toward the player will be a considerable help.

Let's begin with the driver. For purposes of discussion we will assume a wind of twenty miles an hour, which is a speed that nearly every player encounters from time to time, and which is plenty strong to affect every shot hit.

Into a wind of twenty miles an hour the golfer whose average drive with no wind factor is, say, two hundred thirty yards can expect to have his average distance cut down by about thirty yards. (The ratio of 30 to 230 will apply generally.) He should, therefore, base his strategy of play on drives of about two hundred yards. This may seem elementary to the point of laboring the obvious, but the fact is, nevertheless, that the majority of poor drives hit into the wind stem from unwarranted attempts to get as much distance into the wind as would be attained without it. Hence the overswing, the lunge, the ball not solidly hit—in short, the poor drive.

It is not an easy thing to learn to swing with controlled power when the wind is blowing strongly toward you. The natural psychological tendency is to strive for something extra, to try to overcome the effects of that adverse wind by hitting the ball harder than usual. As to this, I can only say the tendency must be overcome, and add some reasons why it must be.

This brings us again to the proposition of keeping spin off the ball when playing into the wind. (Here it might be well to explain that I am advocating not so much that you try consciously to keep spin *off* the ball as that you strive to avoid putting any more than the normal spin on it. I recognize, as I know the reader will, that no shot can become airborne unless it has some underspin on it.) Now, with the driver the surest way to keep extra spin off the ball is to get as much of the club face on the ball at contact as possible. To put it more simply: The idea is to hit the ball as solidly as you can. To this end, you should swing well within your maximum power so as to maintain balance and rhythm (timing).

Often I have heard the advice given that you should make a conscious effort to swing considerably easier than normally when playing into the wind. This advice I regard as sound only insofar as it would tend to produce a normal, controlled-power swing—on the theory that the conscious effort at the easy swing will be balanced against the subconscious tendency to overswing into the wind. What is needed is the same swing that would be sound if we were playing downwind, or with no wind. That is the ideal.

In trying to achieve this ideal, it will help to give some positive thought to the obvious fact that whatever side spin we put on the ball will be considerably accentuated by this twenty-mile wind. Thus, what would with no wind be a small slice or hook becomes a sizable slice or hook when the wind takes hold of that right or left spin and increases it. There is the further fact, which may not be as obvious, that your ball will stay in the air a greater amount of time while travelling a shorter distance when the wind is against you, so that your slice or hook will be more pronounced with reference to the distance covered.

It may be seen, then, that the problems involved in driving into the wind are in the main mental. There is just one physical adjustment I would advocate, and that one principally for advanced players: In taking your stance and throughout your swing, tend to keep more weight on the left heel. This will tend to shorten the swing and prevent the type of arc that sends the ball quickly up. To put it another way, it will help you hit straight through the ball rather than up on it.

For those who naturally hook or slice and always allow for it, I can only advise that you make a greater allowance when the wind is against you. How much greater? Well, with this twenty-mile wind we have assumed, about 20 per cent greater. You will be at a greater disadvantage than ever when the wind is high, and there isn't much you can do about the fact as long as you remain a curve-ball hitter. This is, unfortunately, more particularly true of the slicer, since the left-to-right curve produces a greater amount of underspin than the right-to-left curve.

A word or two about teeing the ball for drives into the wind: I am against teeing it abnormally low. For one thing, you want the ball up high enough to get all of the club face on the ball. For another, teeing the ball very low will tend to produce a more downward blow rather than a level sweep, and the downward blow will produce the greater amount of spin. Neither do I favor teeing it more than ordinarily high, as some few professionals do. My thought here is that you should definitely avoid making it easier to hit the ball on the under side, for obvious reasons.

Moving along to the fairway woods, the same general principles apply as with the drives. One difference will be that it will be necessary, usually, to strike the ball more of a downward blow in order to get it up, and therefore you will put more spin on it. This can hardly be avoided; it simply must be taken into account. Try to catch the ball solidly and with as nearly level a sweep as the lie will permit.

With our twenty-mile wind, distance on fairway woods will be cut down in about the same ratio as with the driver. About the only helpful thing about playing fairway woods into the wind is that it becomes easier to get the ball airborne, for the reason that the wind will begin as soon as the ball leaves the club to increase the underspin and send the ball into the air. It is reasonable to say, with respect to club loft, that a twenty-mile wind will, for practical purposes, make a three-wood of your two-wood and a four-wood of your three-wood.

This wind will almost, in fact, make a two-wood of your driver for purposes of getting the ball into the air. The face loft of a standard driver is eleven degrees, as compared to fourteen degrees for the two-wood, sixteen degrees for the three-wood and nineteen degrees for the four-wood. (The subject of club characteristics is treated more fully in Chapter 2, but these figures are cited here to show it is not unreasonable to use a driver from exceptionally good lies in the fairway when the wind is blowing toward you.) Use of the driver from good lies in the fairway, when that is feasible, will add considerably to your distance playing into a strong wind. The driver, being less lofted, will put less spin on the ball, in addition to producing the leveling-out type of flight that brings so much greater distance into the wind.

To test your lie for the possible use of a driver from the fairway, examine it to be sure the ball is sitting nicely on top of the grass and that you will be able to get virtually all of the club face on the ball with a sweeping type of blow. If the ball is down in the grass at all, resolve all doubt in favor of the two-wood or three-wood. This type of lie makes for distance with a more lofted club anyway, since the grass between the ball and the club face at impact will reduce the spin.

LONG IRONS INTO THE WIND

The long iron shot into a stiff wind is, to my way of thinking, the hardest shot a golfer comes up against in the normal course of play. One factor that makes it tougher than the more lengthy fairway wood shot is the necessity for striking a more descending blow on the iron shot, which puts added spin on the ball. Then there is the fact that the long iron has a very small club face area on which the ball may be struck to produce a good shot—no more than half that of a wood club. It follows from this that any shot hit slightly off center with a long iron will lose much of the power needed to send it through a strong wind, and will likely have some side spin.

135

What is indicated with the long iron, then, is extra care to insure a solidly hit ball, which, as with the wood (or any club), calls for a controlled-power swing. It thus becomes of paramount importance to select a club with which the green may be comfortably reached. Here is no place to try for added distance. If you think you *might* get home with the three-iron, just yank the two-iron out of the bag with the utmost confidence that you are making the right choice of clubs. For one thing, the less lofted club will naturally bring about the lesser amount of spin; for another, you stand a much better chance of catching the ball solidly, because you will be able to concentrate on that objective, to the exclusion of any worry about reaching the green.

In connection with this matter of choosing a club, remember that almost any type of shot hit into a twenty-mile or stronger wind will stop within a few feet after it hits, even on hard green with sparse grass. So the danger of going over the green is minimized.

The player who hits a reasonably straight ball will find that in a twenty-mile wind his two-iron will produce about the same type of shot, both as to distance and flight characteristics, as his four-iron will with no wind factor. This comparison will apply generally

136

down through the rest of the clubs, but it will be of some value to remember that between the two-iron and four-iron lofts there is a difference of six degrees (two-iron 21 degrees and four-iron 27) while between the more lofted clubs, beginning with the five-iron, there is a difference of four degrees for each club.

The player who nearly always hits a left-to-right type of shot (the fader or slicer) will find his into-the-wind distance cut down even more than will the straight-ball hitter, because of that added underspin. The natural hooker will find his distance affected in about the same degree as that of the straight-ball hitter, possibly even a little less because of the added roll a hook tends to produce.

The swing used for playing iron shots into the wind is virtually the same as that used for playing irons under any conditions. So is the stance. My experience has not borne out the often-taught theory that shots into the wind should be played with the ball back nearer the right foot at address. This adjustment does, as its adherents claim, tend to produce a lower trajectory—but it also makes for a more downward or chopping blow, and hence for more spin. My view is that the advantage of the lower trajectory is offset by the added spin, which leaves us with nothing but the handicap of using a somewhat unnatural swing. I do advise added emphasis on keeping the weight through the left heel on into-the-wind iron shots, as with wood shots under the same conditions.

SHORTER IRONS INTO THE WIND

The four-, five-, and six-irons are usually placed in the middle-iron category; the seven-, eight-, and nine-irons are commonly thought of as the short irons. But for into-the-wind shots I would move the six-iron over into the short-iron range. This is perhaps a rather arbitrary distinction, but I make it in order to emphasize a point: Whenever there is a strong wind blowing toward you there is added danger in getting the ball very high, as full shots with clubs of six-iron loft and greater are apt to do.

I have sought to show in the discussion of long-iron play into the wind the importance of swinging well within your maximum power. This principle applies with even greater force as we come to the shorter irons.

As we come to the shorter irons there is great advantage to be derived from playing less-than-full shots. Suppose, for instance, that your ball lies in the fairway ninety yards from the pin, and our assumed twenty-mile wind is blowing straight toward you. You look the shot over and conclude that a full nine-iron shot will produce the needed distance. You start to take out the nine-iron. Don't.

Instead, picture in your mind the likely trajectory a full nine-iron shot will take. Hit normally, the shot will go very high and will be the absolute pawn of the wind gusts because it is sadly lacking in forward power. Any right or left tendency it has will be accentuated by the wind. Further, if it misses the green and lands in a sand trap it will likely bury itself, leaving you what is sometimes called the "fried-egg lie," with your ball playing the part of the yolk.

How much better, then, to play about a three-quarter seven-iron shot in this situation? It figures to be lower, have more forward power to hold its line through the wind, and, as stated before, there is hardly a problem of stopping the ball quickly after it hits when the wind is strong against you. This shot is in all respects the superior shot of the two, and its principles apply on virtually all into-the-wind shots from, say, one hundred thirty yards into the green.

Many players shun the three-quarter swing because they believe themselves prone to miss the shot whenever they "let up." This is taking the wrong view of the shot. It calls not so much for an easy swing as for a short swing—three-quarter length rather than three-quarter power. I would ask a player with the theory stated above whether he would want a club lofted enough to permit a full swing on a simple thirty-yard shot. I feel sure he wouldn't, and I feel equally sure he shouldn't hit a full-power nine-iron on simple shots into a strong wind.

The principles that apply in playing into a twenty-mile wind should carry over very well to winds of other speeds. That speed was selected as a basis for this discussion because it would be strong enough to pose real problems on the various shots, yet not so strong but that a resourceful player could solve the problems and keep his score within a few strokes of his average.

We have seen that a twenty-mile wind will make a difference of about two-clubs on a given shot. It should follow then—and does—that a ten-mile wind should make a one-club difference. A three-club difference for a thirty-mile wind is a fair estimate. Other speeds would be judged in proportion, though it is patently impossible to draw up any exact table, since other factors, such as atmospheric conditions (damp or heavy air will cut down on distance) and expected roll, will make a difference.

When the wind reaches forty miles an hour and upward, normal golf shots are extremely hard to play. Under such conditions resourcefulness and ingenuity play more important roles in keeping scores down. Then it may become expedient to play shots from one hundred or so yards out with a two-iron or three-iron, using a half swing. At times the best results on a fifty- or sixty-yard shot may be obtained by rolling the ball with your putter. Fortunately, little golf is played under such conditions, but if you find yourself in a position of having to do so, do not hesitate to depart from the orthodox.

FOLLOWING WINDS

The problems involved in playing with a following wind are naturally much more simple than those posed by an adverse wind. Not only is the problem of distance simplified, but also that of accuracy. A good brisk following wind will minimize slices and hooks by carrying your ball along with it in the direction of the hole. For another thing, a following wind tends to add to the player's confidence, especially on long shots, and most golfers swing their best with a nice wind at their backs.

My advice is to use your normal swing when playing with a following wind of reasonable proportions. I see no advantage to be gained by making special adjustments in order to get the ball high. The wind speed fifty feet above the ground is not appreciably higher than it is twenty feet above. On iron shots to the green, I am definitely opposed to the practice of trying to impart extra underspin to the ball to cut down on its roll unless that is made necessary by traps or other obstacles guarding the green. It is much better, I find, to try to hit the shot with no more than the normal amount of spin and allow for a normal amount of roll. In that way the judgment of over-all distance, a major problem in playing in a following wind, is made easier.

According to my observations, most golfers believe that the stronger the following wind the farther a given shot will travel in the air. This is not true; and is, I believe, the basis of a lot of incorrect thinking about the effect of following winds in golf. A wind speed of fifteen to twenty miles an hour will produce the maximum carry on a golf shot. To fully understand why, let's go back to our statement about an adverse wind helping to get the ball airborne. Conversely, the following wind keeps the ball down because its continuing effect is to level the ball's flight in conformity with the wind's own movement.

In winds up to about twenty miles an hour the distance that the wind carries the ball along more than offsets the flight lost through this leveling action. But in very strong winds the leveling action keeps the ball from attaining height and the effect is to knock the ball down quickly and reduce carry.

This lesson was brought home forcibly to me a few years ago at the Cypress Point course near San Francisco. I was playing in Bing Crosby's fine tournament with three good players. It was a stormy day, and by the time we reached the 18th the wind was upwards of fifty miles an hour. The first two players to hit used drivers and each caught the ball solidly. But their balls seemed to duck quickly toward the ground, and because the fairway was soggy it yielded little roll and the resulting drives were little if any longer than would have been the case with no wind. The third player, taking a lesson from the first two, hit a three-wood from the tee and passed the first two by some twenty yards. So, becoming more impressed with the wind as each of the three other shots were hit, I took a three-iron out of the bag. I opened the face of the club and hit as much up on the ball as I could so as to get it high quickly. My drive was the longest by fifty yards.

Most golfers will not encounter such a wind in a lifetime of play (it was the strongest I have ever played in, and had it not been tournament play my companions and I would have gone to the clubhouse several holes earlier), but I think it does provide a good, though extreme, example of the effect of a strong following wind on a golf shot. In judging prospective flight, then, be sure to take into account this leveling action. Judgment of roll must, of course, be based on the texture of the ground where the ball will hit, plus the length and thickness of the grass.

To get a good carry, the ball must be hit with enough power to take it up through the wind to a proper height, so be wary of under-clubbing when a strong wind is behind you and distance in the air is needed.

This brings up a question I have often been asked: Will a two-wood or three-wood give more distance off the tee than the driver when the wind is following? My answer in general would be, in winds up to twenty miles an hour, no; in stronger winds, yes. Much depends on the way the ball is hit. Thus a player who habitually hits low balls might be well advised to take a more lofted wood in fifteen-mile winds, while a high ball hitter should stick to the driver through winds of twice that speed.

While a following wind is most helpful in getting distance, it is a considerable handicap on less-than-full shots into the green. This handicap is most pronounced on holes where the green is guarded by traps or elevated on all sides so that the only approach is by air. Here the angle of descent comes strongly into the play, and where there is a following wind this angle of descent is gradual and conducive to roll. The best way around this problem is proper placement of the shot preceding the approach to the green, so as to have the maximum amount of space in which to stop the ball.

The shot that will stop quickest under the conditions outlined above is the full wedge, which will give a maximum height for a sharp angle of descent and a large amount of underspin. Any shot hit less than full is apt to have a lower trajectory and will have a lesser amount of underspin because the inter-action between the club face grooves and the ball is at a maximum only on a full shot. With this in mind, it is often wise to make the tee shot purposely shorter when it can be seen that the second shot on a hole will call for stopping the ball quickly after it hits the green.

On full iron shots into the green there is no wisdom in taking a more lofted club than the shot seems to call for and pressing it for extra distance. A compact, controlled-power swing with the proper club will produce the better stopping action. Such a stroke permits the club face grooves to produce the underspin action for which they are designed.

CROSSWINDS

The problems posed by crosswinds are largely problems of proper aiming. Some better players try to hold a shot straight into a right-to-left wind by deliberately cutting across the ball slightly so as to give it a fading action, and into a left-to-right wind by imparting a slight hook spin. To my mind, this is a needless complicating of the problem, for the simple reason that it calls for more skill and precision than does the simpler method of lining up the shot in accordance with the amount of drift the wind can be expected to produce.

There are too many variable factors to permit setting up a table to show that a shot of a certain length and height will change course so much in a wind of a certain speed. Nor is such a table necessary, in my opinion. Gauging such shots call for the same type of judgment as judging distance on any shot. There are, however, some facts in this connection that are often overlooked. One is that all full shots, from the woods to the short irons, will, with respect to over-all right or left drift, be affected in about the same degree by a given wind. This is because the long shots, having a lot of forward power in the initial stage of flight, will be little affected until near the end, while the short shots, lacking this power and having more spin, can be turned more easily by the wind. But, of course, the long shots are affected by the wind over a greater distance.

The right-handed player, and especially one who tends to hook the ball, finds it very easy to drive when there is a right-to-left crosswind. Such a condition fits right into his natural pattern of play. But the left-to-right wind poses a very difficult driving problem. As for myself, I find it the toughest driving situation of all. To overcome it, I advocate a more than ordinarily careful lining up of the shot plus extra care in making it.

Careful lining up of a shot calls for checking the position of the feet, hips, and shoulders with reference to the intended line. Some golfers will try to line up a shot into a crosswind by simply turning the shoulders slightly, with the feet in the same position as for a straight away shot. Some players, in fact, assume they are aiming a certain way simply because they are looking that way. The best method is to pick out some object to line up on and draw an imaginary line from the object back to your feet. This system will prevent indecisive aiming, the most common fault of the average player when playing into a crosswind. The method will be particularly effective for hookers playing into a strong left-to-right wind. Such players through long habit line up to the right of the objective and find it very hard to change when the situation calls for a change.

QUARTERING WINDS

My own method for playing shots when the wind is quartering against me—that is blowing back and across the line of flight—is to change the position of the club face slightly. If the wind is quartering from the left, I close the face just a degree or two, and if it is quartering from the right I open the face of the club just about the same amount. This adjustment is very slight, and it must be made *before* taking the grip. If the club is toed in or out after you have gripped the club for a straight away shot it will revert to a square position during the course of the swing.

Winds quartering from behind simply call for a slight adjustment in aiming.

○ ○ ○ ○ ○ ○ ○ ○ ○ ○ 10

Round in a Big Wind

IN CONJUNCTION WITH the foregoing chapter
on Wind Play, I offer a description of a competitive
round I played in strong and highly variable winds—
the final round of the 1956 Masters Tournament. It is
not a round I recall with a great deal of pleasure, but I
feel it provides some valuable object lessons relating to
wind play.

My preparations for playing on that very windy day
began on the practice tee with a slight widening of the
stance on all shots. The feet spread farther apart gives

a wider base and hence lessens the chance that you may be blown off balance by the strong wind. Also, the wider stance will reduce the body turn, thus shortening the swing, which is desirable in the wind.

Here on the practice also is where the mental preparations begin. I tried to concentrate with added intensity on hitting the ball solidly on the middle of the club face, and I tried to condition my mind to swinging well within my full power, knowing that the adverse winds out on the course would tempt me to try to get something extra into the shot to compensate for the strong wind coming into me. I tried to determine also that I was going to be patient out on the course, because I knew from experience that the shot problems were going to be more difficult and would require more calm and ordered judgment than would be the case under normal conditions.

On the practice putting green, I gave extra attention to trying to perfect my touch for distance, because I knew the greens would be getting drier, harder, and slicker as the hard wind continued to blow over them. I putted about a dozen extra short putts, downhill and with the grain of the grass, tapping the ball very easy and trying to determine whether the wind would alter the course of the ball as it was rolling along. Sometimes it would and sometimes it wouldn't, the wind being that variable.

A few minutes before my tee time I reviewed in my mind the various problems that I knew would be coming up. I made a mental note that I would be playing, in effect, a very different golf course than the Augusta National usually is, and I tried to determine that I would be more on the alert than ordinarily to try to cope with these different situations.

The wind that Sunday afternoon was blowing at a minimum of about thirty-five miles per hour and there were frequent gusts up to about fifty miles per hour. Tornado warning had been issued for a number of towns near Augusta, Georgia, where the Masters is played over the Augusta National Golf Club. This was the second day in a row that the wind had blown very strong, with the result that the big, rolling greens had been thoroughly dried out and were hard and fast. The greens themselves were cut very close for this final day of play, and in a number of instances the wind would actually alter the course of a putt while it was rolling.

My personal situation was that I was in second place in the tournament, four strokes behind Ken Venturi, the fine San Francisco player who seemed about to become the first amateur ever to win the Masters.

Doug Ford, my playing partner, and I were to go out fifteen minutes ahead of Venturi, which meant that he would have whatever advantages accrued from knowing what he needed to do to protect his lead over me. My thought was that 71 or 72 would be about the best round shot by anybody that day, conditions being what they were. I determined that my strategy would be simply to make as many pars as possible, hoping for a 72 and figuring that if that were not good enough I just couldn't win. With all that wind, and with the difficult pin placements, I think the conditions that day were as tough as any I have ever played under.

Number 1—The first hole at Augusta is four hundred yards. The big wind was mostly from left to right, but quartering slightly against us. The pin was in the back right corner of the green. I concentrated on getting my driver solidly on the ball, aiming just to the left of the center of the fairway and figuring that if the wind carried my ball to the right side it would be all to the good as far as my second shot was concerned. I got off a good drive. Looking over my second shot, I thought I could probably reach the green with a strong five-iron, but decided on an easy four-iron with the thought of keeping the ball lower and keeping the spin off it. That shot came off well, leaving me a thirty-foot putt from the right side of the green, and I holed it for a birdie-three.

Number 2—This one is 527 yards, par-five. The wind was nearly dead against us, but the drive here is protected from the wind by woods on each side. I was able to get a little more than 250 yards off the tee. From that point the hole dog-legs sharply to the left, so that the wind was helping some. I hit a fine two-iron that rolled through the small opening on to the green and stopped forty feet from the flag, which was in the left hand corner. My first putt was a good ten feet short, but I got the next one in to go two under.

Number 3—On this 370-yard par-four, the wind was again almost square in our faces. Again I concentrated heavily on getting the ball solidly on the face of my driver and got off a good drive. For the second shot here, the wind blowing toward you is a blessing, since one of the second-shot problems on this hole is stopping the ball after it hits on this wide but shallow green. From about 140 yards out, I hit a good, hard five-iron shot—and had three different ideas about the shot before it hit. At first it seemed the ball would carry over the green . . . then the wind caught it good and it looked like it might settle right on the pin . . .

then the wind kept kicking it higher and higher, and eventually it settled on the front edge. From thirty feet, I got down in two putts for a par. Still two under.

Number 4—Waiting on the tee of this 220-yard par-three, I saw a score board that showed Venturi had started 5-5 against my 3-4, meaning I was only one stroke back. With no wind, this hole plays about a two-iron, but into that wind it looked like a good strong driver shot. I gave some thought to hitting my three-wood, but I knew a shot with this club would be apt to get very high, and I feared that if it was a little short it would be coming straight down and would bury in the sand (the pin was placed right behind a deep sand trap). I knew the wind was gusty and changing, but as I hit the shot with my driver it seemed to be blowing strong and steady. The ball took off on a good line for the pin. I was most happy with it until the wind suddenly slowed and I saw it was well over. It was so far over, in fact, that it would have been out of bounds had it not been for some thick bushes and a fence about twenty yards behind the green. The fence stopped it. I made my way through the bushes, found the ball barely playable, got it out short of the green but out of the bushes, then all but holed a chip shot with my pitching wedge. A bogey four and very happy to have it. Probably a two-wood would have been the club for this hole, but I was not carrying one.

Number 5—This 460-yard par-four was the first of three disastrous holes for me that day. My drive, with the wind blowing from right to left, was a big one. The hole is a slight dog-leg to the left, which meant the wind was helping some on the second shot, but that also meant I could hardly hope to stop the ball if I made it hit on the top level of the green where the pin was. I hit a four-iron purposely short of the green and the ball rolled nicely on to the front edge, maybe thirty feet short. The first putt had to go up the bank to the top level of the green, but it was not a difficult one. I left it three feet short in what looked like good position. When I looked at my putt for my par I could not be sure in my mind whether there was a break to be played. So I examined the cup itself and it seemed to be definitely higher on the left, indicating a break to the right. I played a break to the right. It wasn't there, apparently, and the ball ran two feet past. Again I thought I saw a break, played a break, and missed again. By the time I got down the next one from a foot, what had looked like an easy par had turned into a terrible double bogey six. It shook me.

Number 6—This one is 190 yards, par-three. I hit

a wonderful looking five-iron shot that nearly hit in the hole and stopped four feet past. I hit the putt for a birdie-two the way I thought I wanted to, but it stayed out. I tapped it in for a par to stay one over.

Number 7—On this 370-yard par-four I hit one of my very few wild tee shots of the tournament, one that would have been well to the right of the fairway had it not caught in the top of a pine tree and dropped below it in the edge of the fairway. There were overhanging limbs that made it necessary to keep the ball very low, so I played a half-four-iron shot that ended at the base of the narrow pathway up to the elevated, small green. Then came a shot that would have shamed any 100-shooter you know: In trying to pitch into the fringe at the top of the pathway, I scuffed the shot, hit it weakly, and it ended up six feet to the left of my hip pocket and in the sand trap. My sand shot was a good one, four feet past the hole, but I missed the putt and there was another double-bogey—the second one in three holes.

Number 8—This one is a par-five, 525 yards. I pushed another drive into the edge of the rough, came out well enough with a two-iron, and hit an eight-iron shot fifteen feet from the hole. The putt was close, and I tapped the next one in for a par.

Number 9—The wind was helping on this 420-yard par-four, and I got off a long and well-placed drive. My second shot with an eight-iron was on the pin all the way, halting no more than six inches from the hole. I tapped that one in for a birdie-three to finish the nine with a two-over-par 38.

Number 10—This hole is rightfully called one of the best and prettiest to be found anywhere. It measures 470 yards, but is mostly downhill, and is a par-four. I hit one of the longest drives of the day. For my second shot, I picked a seven-iron, which probably wasn't enough. At any rate, I failed to get the ball high enough, and left it ten yards short of the green. From there I chipped eight feet past with a pitching wedge and missed coming back to take a bogey.

Number 11—This is a very tough hole, 460 yards and par-four. The tee shot comes out of the woods and is rather well protected from the wind. Mine was long and straight. The green is guarded on the left side by a pond, and the flag was set right back of that pond. With a three-iron, I aimed thirty feet to the right of the pin, away from the pond, and hit the shot just as planned. Two putts gave me an easy par. Still three over.

Number 12—This one is about 165 yards long

with the pin in the back right corner of the green, as it was on this day. It is protected on three sides by tall trees, which probably accounts for its being the trickiest hole on the course when the wind is high and gusty. Earlier, Bob Rosburg had hit a four-iron on the hole and, when the wind died suddenly as the ball was in flight, saw it sail over a thirty-foot high bank back of the green and into the Augusta Country Club Course —out of bounds. Then the wind came back and he hit the same kind of shot. It stopped ten feet from the hole and he made the putt for a bogey four.

The day before, in about the same kind of wind, I had hit a five-iron to the top of that bank, nearly out of bounds. This time I hit a good five-iron and it was short, stopping on the bank of the little creek that flows in front of the green. The next one was a good pitch six feet away, and I made it for a par.

Number 13—This par-five hole, which has decided a number of Masters tournaments, is a left dog-leg that plays about 475 yards if you stay about in the middle of the fairway. I hit a fair drive, played the second shot safely short of the creek bordering the green, and got a simple par-five by pitching up and two-putting from twelve feet.

Number 14—Here the wind was almost straight

behind us. The hole is a fairly simple par-four, measuring 390 yards. My drive was a long one. I took a nine-iron for my second, hoping to hit just short of the green and bounce on. But I failed to get height on the ball quickly enough, and the strong following wind leveled out the flight and brought the ball down too quickly, short of the putting surface by a few feet. I used my putter for the third shot, got it up within five feet, and made the putt for a par.

Number 15—On this 470-yard par-five, famous for the Sarazen double eagle, I hit a good drive into the wind, played safely short of the water with a three-iron, made rather a poor pitch shot, and two-putted from thirty-five feet for a par-five.

Number 16—This par-three hole over the water most of the way plays about 195 yards. I hit a four-iron, deliberately hooking it a little to try to get close to the pin, which was in the far left corner of the green. The shot came off well, stopping about twenty-five feet away. The first putt slid by a little, and I made the next one for a par.

Number 17—This one is 380 yards, par-four, and again the wind was following. A scoreboard is situated by the tee. I checked it and found that Venturi was playing rather badly, and decided that if I could

finish with a birdie and a par I might win the tournament. My drive was long and straight, leaving me a
shot of about 135 yards. The pin was on the front right
of the green, behind a trap. That meant it would be
tough, with that following wind, to stop the ball near
the cup. I decided to hit a soft eight-iron shot with as
much spin as I could get on the ball, cutting it a little
to produce a left-to-right flight. I cut it a little too
much, the wind knocked it down some, and it hit the
top of the bank, kicked right away from the trap, and
wound up at the base of the bank of the green. My
pitch with a wedge went six feet by.

At this point, though I could not possibly have
known it, I was probably putting to win the tournament. But in any event, I hit what I took to be a good
putt. A foot short of the hole the ball veered slightly
to the left when a wind gust swept the green, and the
ball trickled on two and a half feet past the hole. Then
I missed that one coming back, and my third double-
bogey of the day was on the card.

Number 18—On this par-four finishing hole, I hit
a good drive, followed by a seven-iron shot fifteen feet
from the hole. A routine two-putt green gave me a par
and a score of 77, for a total of 291 for the 72 holes.

It was not until an hour later, after Jack Burke, the

eventual winner, and Venturi, had finished, that I could comprehend that the double-bogey on 17 had been so costly. Burke, playing two sets behind me, had birdied the 17th with a great sixteen-foot putt. Then his second shot on 18 had wound up in a trap in front of the green, from which spot he had blasted out beautifully and holed a three-footer for a par and a winning 289. Venturi finished with an 80 for 290.

Had I made a simple par on No. 17, as I almost surely could have done by playing the second shot safely on to the green instead of trying to cut it close for a birdie, I would have had a 75 and a 290 total. That, as it turned out, would have beaten Venturi by a stroke. Then, when Burke was in the sand in two at No. 18 he would have known he had to get down in two from there to tie me, instead of knowing that he could get down in three and still beat me for the top professional prize (at the time it still looked like Venturi would be the winner).

Burke is, of course, a fine and resourceful golfer, and might very well have got down from the sand in two under any circumstances. But the situation would have been a different one, and so might have been his reaction to it. Thus we find a lesson here in that it is never wise to assume too much about what the other fellow may do—we should always give ourselves the best chance by trying to play good, sound golf whatever the situation.

There is another lesson to be learned from the 5th hole. When the putt for a par failed to break and missed the hole, I should have assumed that the one coming back wouldn't break either. After all, I was putting both times on the same small area of green. And I knew, as set forth in Chapter 4, that a putt coming back to the hole will usually follow the same line it took after it passed the hole.

My conduct on the 7th hole, where I hit a childishly simple little pitch shot into a trap, must have been traceable to the four-putt green two holes back. The lesson: when a hole is finished, that's all—put it out of your mind and play the following holes as best you can. This is not always psychologically possible, even for the most experienced players, but it is the ideal that must be striven for.

Twice—on the 14th and 17th holes—I failed to take properly into account that a strong following wind will level out the flight of a shot and reduce the carry unless the ball is hit so as to attain height quickly.

On the 4th hole, where my shot with the driver carried well over the green, I probably was guilty of a mistake in judgment. Certainly I knew the wind to be gusty, and since my equipment did not include a two-wood, which would have been ideal for this particular shot, I doubtless should have used the three-wood and aimed for a part of the green not guarded by the front trap.

These are the mistakes I made that day in the wind. I hope you can profit by studying them.

○ ○ ○ ○ ○ ○ ○ ○ ○ ○ ○ 11

Wet Weather Play

IN THE FINAL ROUND of the 1956 Bing Crosby
Tournament I played the famous Pebble Beach
Course in 68 shots and won the event with a record-
setting score of 202 for the 54 holes. I thought at the
time that it was probably the finest round I had ever
played. What made it remarkable was the conditions
under which it was played. Pebble Beach, a tough
and testing golf course in the fairest of weather, had
been rained on for days and was very soggy, and it

rained throughout the round I am describing. Further, it was a day of strong and variable winds.

The day was, in short, the kind that made it possible for me to put to use about everything my experience as a playing professional had taught me about playing in wet weather. So I feel that by detailing the preparations and play of that particular day I can impart to the reader as much as I know about wet weather play. Some of the preparations and precautions may be more elaborate than the average amateur will care to make and take, but I offer them as useful aids for whatever times you may find yourself in the position of wanting to hold your golf score to a minimum on a rainy day. I shall describe the things that went into the playing of that round, leaving it to the reader to relate them to his own particular problem.

Against the rainy, chilly weather, I put on two cashmere sweaters over a long-sleeved golf shirt, rain pants over regular golf slacks, and regular golf shoes over heavy socks. I chose a cap with a longer than ordinary bill to insure that the driving rain wouldn't get to my eyes while I was over a shot, and I took along a pair of plain sun glasses to put on when I had an iron shot from a close lie and feared I might splatter mud in my eye in taking a divot. (Once that happens, you may easily begin flinching on subsequent iron shots, with dire results. I used the glasses on six shots during the day.) And I took along two extra dry gloves.

Then I told my caddy what I expected of him for the day. I told him that if the grips on my clubs got wet I wouldn't be able to play at all, and it would cost considerable money. I instructed him to keep the hood of the bag zipped up half way and over the club heads at all times, with a heavy bath towel over the hood. Another towel was to be carried in the ribs of our umbrella, which he was to carry. (Carrying a heavy umbrella may tend to stiffen your wrist after so long a time.)

Next I reviewed in my mind the golf rule applying to casual water. This rule is all-important when playing in the rain or after a heavy rain. It was written into the rules to keep the standing water from imposing unfair penalties on the player, and every fair advantage should be taken of its provisions. Here is the definition of casual water:

"CASUAL WATER" IS ANY TEMPORARY ACCUMULATION OF WATER WHICH IS NOT A HAZARD OF ITSELF OR WHICH IS NOT IN A WATER HAZARD. SNOW AND ICE ARE "CASUAL WATER" UNLESS OTHERWISE DETERMINED BY LOCAL RULE.

Here is the rule (No. 32) covering casual water:

1. BALL LYING IN OR TOUCHING—*If a player's ball lies in or touches casual water, ground under repair, or hole, cast or runway made by a burrowing animal, a reptile or a bird, the player may obtain relief as follows:*

   a. Through the green—*Through the green, the player may lift and drop the ball without penalty as near as possible to the spot where it lay, but not nearer the hole, on ground which avoids these conditions.*

   b. In a hazard—*In a hazard, the player may lift and drop the ball either:—Without penalty, in the hazard as near as possible to the spot where the ball lay, but not nearer the hole, or ground which affords maximum relief from these conditions.*

   OR

   Under penalty of one stroke, outside the hazard as near as possible to the spot where the ball lay, but not nearer the hole.

   c. On the putting green—*On the putting green, or if such conditions intervene be-*

tween a ball lying on the putting green and the hole, the player may lift the ball and place it without penalty in the nearest position to where it lay which affords a maximum relief from these conditions, but no nearer the hole.

2. INTERFERENCE—*If any of the conditions covered by this rule interfere with the player's stance, or the backward movement of his club for the stroke, the ball may be treated as in Clause 1.*

3. BALL LOST—*If a ball be lost under a condition covered by this rule, a ball may be dropped without penalty as near as possible to the place where the ball entered the area, on ground which avoids these conditions, but not nearer the hole. In order that a ball may be treated as lost, there must be reasonable evidence to that effect.*

4. RE-DROPPING—*If a ball, when dropped, rolls into a position covered by this rule, it may be re-dropped without penalty. If it be impossible to drop a ball so that it will not roll into such condition, it shall be placed.*

PENALTY FOR BREACH OF RULE:
Match-play—Loss of hole; *Stroke-play*—Two strokes.

I quote the basic provisions of this rule in full because I think many players fail to understand some of its more important sections. Virtually all golfers know they are permitted under the rule to move a ball without penalty out of any temporary accumulation of water on the course, but it is not nearly so well understood that the rule makes it unnecessary to putt the ball through standing water on the green. And probably less than half the average players know they can move the ball without penalty to keep from having to stand in casual water in making the shot.

I think it will be seen from a study of this rule that its clear intent is to make a rain-soaked golf course *fair* to all concerned, so that it will continue to reward accuracy, distance, good judgment, and touch.

I next sought to evaluate the situation in which I found myself at the start of the round, and to make some determination of the general strategy I would use in the play. I was tied for the lead with Bob Rosburg of San Francisco, and Mike Souchak of Pittsburgh was a stroke behind. The rest of the field was pretty well strung out behind us three. I knew Rosburg and Souchak to be good, strong players, and I was sure I would have to play a sound round of golf to beat them. Further, I felt that a good solid round of golf would beat the rest of the field as well, since Pebble Beach is not a course that lends itself to really phenomenal scores, especially on a rainy and windy day.

I gave some thought to the fact that although a very wet golf course presents some tough problems to the player, it also offers certain advantages: The ball will stop quickly after hitting the green, making for bolder play; putts can be struck more boldly since the wet green is slower and the chance of going well past the hole is lessened; whatever grain* there is in the green will be virtually eliminated when the grass is soaked; judgment of distance on both long shots and putts is easier when there is no glare from the sun; and some drives headed for the rough will hold the fairway because of the lack of roll.

Considering all the facts I could muster, I felt that a 72, or even par, would win for me. (As it turned out, that estimate was exactly right; Souchak shot a 72, and finished second, five strokes back of me, with my 68.)

Out on the practice tee for the warm up, I began

---

* See Chapter 4.

making the small swing adjustments I have found to be helpful in wet weather play: I use a slightly wider stance than my normal one so as to afford myself better footing and cut down on body turn (you are more apt to slip when the ground under you is soft); I leave my left heel solidly on the ground throughout the swing on all shots up through a five-iron, and I lift it only slightly on the longer shots (I lift my left heel as little as possible at all times, but this is especially important to avoid shifting when the ground is soft and wet); and I concentrate more than ever on *hitting the ball first* on all iron shots (any time you hit even slightly behind the ball when the ground is water-soaked you have just about ruined a shot). The chief effect of these adjustments is to swing a little more flat-footed than usual, thus virtually immobilizing the lower half of the body and reducing the chance of having the feet change position during the swing.

One further fact about my golf swing: I tend to pick the ball more cleanly off the turf on iron shots than most other players, which is an especial advantage on wet, soft golf courses. Those players who, as the saying goes, take a divot big enough to bury a dog in, have it tougher when the turf is soaked. A mouthful or an eyeful of mud (or both) is often the reward for taking a big, deep divot from a soaked fairway.

Now come along with me, if you will, for the entire round. I think the value of many of these wet-weather tips will become more apparent as you follow the play. I think, moreover, that you will enjoy the round. I know I did.

NO. 1

The 1st hole at Pebble Beach is 390 yards, par-four. It lies straight away, and no particular trouble threatens so long as you keep to the fairway. I hit a good straight drive that came off the clubhead with that very pleasant feel that accompanies a golf shot solidly hit. I stuck the driver quickly back into the bag to be sure the grip didn't get wet, and I took off my glove and stuck it in my pocket to be sure *it* didn't get wet. (I follow the practice of removing my glove after each shot when it is raining. On dry days I take off my glove only for putting.)

Looking over my second shot, I felt I could reach the green with a hard five-iron shot. I chose, however, to play the shot low with a four-iron, relying on the soft green to hold. I hit the shot just about as planned. It hit the green very near the hole, took one longish hop, and stopped twenty feet past. (It is characteristic of low shots that they will take one long hop and then stop dead after hitting on grass that is covered or virtually covered with water. This applies on short shots as well as full shots.) I two-putted routinely from the twenty feet and had an easy par-four.

NO. 2

The 2nd hole is a good but not especially hard par-five, just under five hundred yards long. Most long hitters can reach it in two shots on a dry day when there is roll to be had, but few can reach it in two when the ground is soggy. A good drive left me with a choice of whether to gamble on carrying over a series of bunkers about seventy-five yards short of the green. I elected to try it, and a good three-wood shot put me about ten yards short of the green in easy chipping position. My wedge chip was four feet from the pin . . . I holed the putt for a birdie-four. Now I had stroke margin on my schedule of par.

NO. 3

The 3rd hole is 375 yards, par-four. It dog-legs sharply to the left, and deep bunkers guard the left side of the fairway to make it a sporting proposition for those who wish to try to save yardage by hugging the left side. I hit a good, safe drive. Here I made one of my two errors of the day. Despite the adverse wind, the shot looked to me like no more than a good five-iron. I hit a good five-iron, and it turned out simply to be not enough club. The shot buried in the bunker just short of the green. From there I made a good sand shot and left the ball six feet from the cup. I hit the putt well, as I thought, but I played too much break. The bogey put me back to even par.

Two lessons on wet weather play are, I think, implicit in the play of this hole. One follows from the play of the second shot: When the rain is coming down the air is likely to be quite heavy, reducing carry to a considerable extent, so you should make very sure you have enough club in your hand—as I did not. Lesson two, from the putt: The ball is apt to break less than it appears it will when the grass is saturated with water, the reason being that the water will help hold the ball on the line it is started on.*

NO. 4

The 4th hole, 350 yards and par-four, is not one of Pebble Beach's more demanding ones. I was able to play it routinely with a drive, a nine-iron to within fifteen feet of the hole, and two putts. The first putt looked like a simple one to either make or get close to the hole, but I continued my practice of closely examining the line between my ball and the cup. It can easily happen on these rainy days that slight extra accumulation of water can go unnoticed on the green and cause you to leave the ball embarrassingly short. Conversely, some small portion of the green can drain more quickly than you would think, with the result that you hit the putt well past the hole. These things must be watched constantly on wet greens.

NO. 5

The 5th hole is a one-shotter, 170 yards long. My five-iron from the tee stopped eight feet past the hole

* See Chapter 4.

and slightly to the left. The putt I had left was over
what is normally the fastest part of the green, and although I examined the line closely and found that part
of the green to be pretty thoroughly saturated, I could
not bring myself to hit the putt quite hard enough. It
was right on the line, but a half inch short. Still on
schedule at even par.

NO. 6

This one stretches out 530 yards and is, naturally,
par-five. Two solid wood shots that stopped right
where they hit left me with a nine-iron shot to the
green. I hit that one twelve feet from the pin, in good
putting position. The putt went right in the middle of
the cup, and I was able to tell myself, as it did so, that
I was beginning to adjust my touch to the wet greens.
One under par now, and ahead of schedule.

NO. 7

The 7th is a little thing, just 115 yards down the
hill. By this time the wind had died down from about
twenty-five to about five miles an hour and the rain
was coming almost straight down instead of driving.

My nine-iron shot left me eight feet from the cup. The putt I had left would normally break about two inches, but because of the water on the green I cut that allowance roughly in half. I stroked the putt, and a pleasant "plop" that followed told me I had gauged it right. Two under.

NO. 8

Walking to the 8th tee, I knew I was about to come face to face with the two most dangerous holes in this golf course. On this one you have to cross a bit of the Pacific Ocean, and on the one that follows you have to skirt that body of water. Re-examining my situation in the light of my two-under-par position, I felt that if I could play No. 8 and No. 9 in a total of no more than nine strokes (one over par for the two holes), I would be in excellent position beginning the back nine. No. 8 is 440 yards, par-four. A good drive left me within three-iron range of the green. This hole is so laid out that the second shot can be played safely to the left of the green—away from the ocean. On a normal day, however, this type of second shot will leave you with a third shot that calls for a chip or a very long putt over a part of the green that is so fast that it becomes virtually impossible to get the ball close. But the rain's having slowed down the green, I was able to take this safe route, and my chip shot left me an easy putt for my par.

NO. 9

The 9th hole is 445 yards, par-four, and a very tough hole. I played a drive and a three-wood to within thirty feet of the pin. Looking along the line of the putt, I could see that there was a heavy accumulation of water in a number of spots. I came very near to asking for a ruling of "casual water intervening between my ball and the cup," which, provided the official agreed, would have permitted me to have moved the ball so as to be able to putt over a drier line. I didn't—and soon wished that I had. My first putt sizzled along throwing up water, and stopped six feet short. My second likewise as to the water, and an inch short.

No one familiar with Pebble Beach will, I think, be astonished when I say I was eminently satisfied with my one-under-par 35 for the first nine. The play up to that point, besides placing me in fine position to win the tournament, convinced me that I was hitting the ball very well and gave me a great deal of confidence for the nine that lay ahead.

NO. 10

The opening hole on Pebble Beach's back nine is 400 yards, par-four. The fairway slopes away toward the ocean on the right, which meant that the left side was relatively high and dry. With confidence based on preceding accuracy from the tee, I aimed down this high left side of the fairway and got excellent distance with my drive. A good seven-iron shot left me seven feet from the pin. The putt seemed to have a break of about three inches to the left. Allowing for a little less than two inches and relying on the wet grass to help the ball hold its line, I made the putt dead center. Back to two under par.

NO. 11

I walked to the 11th tee in pleasant contemplation of the fact that I was two strokes ahead of the scoring schedule I had hoped to maintain and had no more ocean to contend with until the 17th hole. No. 11 is

just under four hundred yards, par-four. A big drive
and an eight-iron second put me ten feet from the
hole. The putt was in from the start. Now three under par.

NO. 12

This one is 210 yards, par-three, with sand guarding all but the right one-third of the green. I hit a hard
two-iron to within thirty feet of the hole, and missed
holing that long one by no more than an inch.

NO. 13

No. 13 is 395 yards, par-four, and lies uphill most
of the way. I followed a straight drive with a straighter
six-iron shot that hit the cup on the first hop, spun out,
and stopped four feet away. My putt broke more than
I figured it would and stayed out on the right side,
bringing me to the realization that the rain had slowed
enough to permit the greens to drain, with the result
that the putts were breaking almost their normal
amount.

NO. 14

On this very long (595 yards) par-five hole I hit a drive and a three-wood to within easy nine-iron distance. My third with that club was five feet from the hole. Taking a lesson from the putt on the hole I had just left, I played almost the full manifest break and made this putt to go four under par.

NO. 15

This one offers a blind tee shot over and down a hill. It is 420 yards, par-four. Here I hit the best tee shot of the day—a day on which all of my tee shots were at or near my best. A seven-iron second shot wound up eighteen feet from the cup. Two putts got me a par.

NO. 16

As I reached the tee for the 16th, the wind had increased and was back up to about twenty miles an hour, and the rain was still coming down. The hole is a slight dog-leg to the right, 380 yards long, and a par-four. The fairway is wide enough to allow lots of room for a safe tee shot to the left, and I played it plenty safe. My second was with a four-iron and was safely on the green. My approach putt was two feet away. It tapped in for a par.

NO. 17

The ocean looms up again at the 220-yard, par-three, 17th. The wind was against me and I had no fear of going over the green even with a driver. But I chose the three-wood for safety's sake, caught the shot solidly in the center of the club face, and was on the green twenty feet from the cup. Two putts again and a par.

NO. 18

The finishing hole at Pebble Beach is a 575-yard, par-five that dog-legs a little to the left and skirts the ocean all the way to the green. I took aim on two pine trees that stand in a safe part of the fairway and my tee shot stopped where it hit some five yards short of the trees. A three-wood shot got me safely by the trees and to within an easy eight-iron shot of the hole. My third

was fifteen feet away. By then I knew where I stood—
five shots ahead of Souchak, who had the score nearest
mine. Perhaps a little over-exuberant, I sent the first
putt five feet by the hole, but made it coming back for
a par-five, a 68, a total for the 54 holes of 202, and a
new scoring record for the tournament. All very nice.

SUMMING UP

I am convinced that we can learn as much about
playing golf from our successes as from our mistakes.
The trouble is, I think, that we do not appraise our
successes as closely as we do our mistakes—which is, of
course, human nature. We tend to accept our best
rounds as simply what we are really capable of doing
at all times, with seldom a thought to going back over
them for the purpose of finding out and remembering
what it was that made us so good on that particular
day.

With this in mind, then, let's look back on this
good round of mine to see what there was about it that
will be helpful to remember. For one thing, I made
careful preparation for it, physically and mentally. I
have, I assure you, played some bad rounds in the rain,
and most of them I could trace to inadequate prepara-

tion and forethought. I have carried a heavy umbrella until my right wrist stiffened and cost me shots—I have had caddies who let the grips of my clubs get wet, simply because I neglected to give them the proper instructions before we started—I have allowed myself to be caught out on the course in the rain without a dry golf glove, which, in combination with wet grips, renders any golfer pretty helpless who is used to wearing a glove—I have cost myself strokes through careless failure to invoke the rule on casual water, largely because I didn't know the rule, but only thought I did—I have hit bad golf shots because I tried to take a full turn with uncertain footing—I have gotten an eye full of mud through hitting just a little behind the ball on an iron shot from a water-logged fairway, and spent the rest of the day flinching from every full iron shot.

I have, in short, made just about all the moist mistakes there are to make, including, lest we forget, knocking an approach putt less than halfway to the hole because I didn't see (didn't look for, either) water half hidden on the green. But on this particular round, I was alert and thinking.

Note that I was patient enough to be able to make corrections for minor errors as I went along, without going to the other extreme. After choosing the wrong iron for my second shot on the 3rd hole, I was not again guilty of under-clubbing myself. Three make-able putts were missed on the first nine because I underestimated the amount of water on the greens, but I used these early experiences in making putts on the 10th and 11th holes. Then on the 13th, after the rain had slackened, I missed a four-footer because I *over*estimated the amount of water on the green and failed to allow for enough break, but I took that lesson quickly to heart and holed a nice putt on the 14th by playing almost the full amount of apparent break.

One other hint about playing in the rain: As soon as you finish your round see that your clubs get imme-diate attention. Take them all out of the bag and dry them thoroughly, paying particular attention to the grips and to the wooden clubheads. Leaving head covers on wet woods overnight will cause the head to swell and split. Your shoes, too, should be wiped dry immediately, and polished after they are dry.

○ ○ ○ ○ ○ ○ ○ ○ ○ ○ ○ ○ ○ *12*

Cold Weather Play

GOLFERS are of several minds as to the degree of temperature at which it becomes "too cold for golf." Some think it is down around zero, or lower; others tend to prefer the clubhouse to the golf course any time the mercury drops below 50. But the fact remains that much golf is played in cold weather. Maybe those who like it cold are highly persuasive and those who like it hot are easily led.

I myself have played a few dozen rounds in extremely cold weather. Sometimes it was by choice, and other times it was because a tournament sponsor had the bad luck to schedule his event to coincide with what turned out to be "the coldest week in this city's history." At any rate, a few observations on cold weather play would seem to be in order.

The first consideration, obviously, is to dress in such a way as to combine comfort and freedom of movement. In this connection, two or more layers of clothes are far better than wearing something thick, as most everybody knows. Those little handwarmers, first introduced to the sporting public by duck hunters, are excellent aids.

My own preparatory tactics call for taking along four or five extra golf balls which I keep close to my body, changing balls at the start of each hole. It is a proven fact that a golf ball travels farther and reacts best when its temperature is 87 degrees. They are made that way.

If the ground is frozen, you will find playing conditions strongly similar to those that obtain in the hot part of the summer when the ground is baked. There is this chief difference: the greens will be considerably slower. Playing on frozen ground, you will be unwise to try to take much of a divot on your iron shots. The unyielding turf will bounce your club back out of it, and the results are apt to be a poor shot and stinging hands.

So try to pick the ball cleanly off the turf with a sweeping stroke. Use a firmer grip to keep from hurting your hands in the event you do take more turf than you expected to. To aid in making your stroke of the sweeping kind, position the ball at address a little further forward toward the right toe than you ordinarily would.

Frozen ground virtually eliminates all chance of stopping the ball quickly after it hits; it will keep hopping and rolling just as it does on baked out turf. No green that is even slightly frozen is apt to be true, so putting will be difficult. It will help your putting to remember that on frozen greens the ball will ride along the top of the grass rather than through the grass, so allow for the maximum amount of break that you see.

Sand

THERE CAN HARDLY BE a more mortifying, annoying, and score-building shot in golf than the one that travels from one spot in a sand trap to another spot in the same trap. A close rival of this one for the dubious honor of being the worst shot in golf is the sand shot that takes off on a hard line and clears the green with room to spare. A terrible feature of these two shots is that they frequently come to rest in positions worse than the ones from which they started. These shots too often provide foundations for those terrible scores on a single hole—eights and nines and higher.

They are shots that I know a great deal about. Even after I began to make a comfortable living and built a fairly formidable reputation as a professional golfer, I hit a lot of these shots. They afflicted me periodically. One week I might be playing sand shots beautifully, then I would mysteriously lose the technique and find myself living in sheer terror of the sand —a far inferior sand player to the average 100-shooter.

It was during one of the sand slumps that, in desperation, I set about to learn the basic facts of sand play and thus gain some consistency. This chapter describes what I found out.

The first step in learning to get the ball near the hole from a sand trap near the green—and this applies to all golfers regardless of ability—is to learn to get the ball *out* of the trap and *somewhere* on the green. By that is meant that you must first develop a safe, basic shot for getting out of the trap from a normal lie in the sand. That accomplished, it becomes possible to develop a sort of touch on the shot that will sometimes enable you to get from the sand trap into a one-putt position.

The best shot for getting out of a sand trap safely

is the full-explosion shot (a full shot in which the club never hits the ball). At times it may be expedient to play a semi-explosion, chip the ball out, or roll it out with your putter. But to repeat, the best and safest shot is the explosion. It is best and safest for the simple reason that it provides the greatest margin for error. By explosion shot I mean the type of shot in which the clubhead makes no direct contact with the ball, but rather with the sand around the ball.

Any discussion of how the explosion shot is played should begin, I believe, with the statement that the shot should be played with the club designed for that specific purpose—the sand wedge. The most important distinguishing feature of the sand wedge is that it has a protruding flange on the bottom that, with a normal swing, will strike the sand *before* any other part of the club does. This flange, with its rounded bottom, will sink only a short distance into the sand and will tend to correct an imperfect swing by causing the clubhead to bounce on through the sand and lift the ball out on the green. To test your sand wedge to see if it is a proper instrument for playing explosion shots, set it down on a floor and observe the bottom of the clubface. With the club square to what would be the intended line of flight, the bottom of the clubface should lack about an eighth to a sixteenth of an inch being flush with the floor.

With the proper club, not much more is needed to play an explosion shot than to swing with about three-quarter power, hit about two inches behind the ball, keep the head stationary, and follow through. Such a stroke will almost invariably produce a lofted shot that will travel about thirty to one hundred feet in the air and stop quickly after it hits.

Recommended refinements to this basic pattern include:

1. *A slightly open stance with feet fairly wide apart (about the width of the shoulders).*
2. *Feet dug into the sand far enough to provide a firm footing throughout the swing.*
3. *Ball positioned about on a line with the left instep.*
4. *A fairly quick breaking of the wrists and hands on the backswing.*
5. *A downswing that sends the hands out in front of the left arm, as in trying to obtain added loft on a pitch shot.*
6. *A consistently firm grip throughout.*
7. *To provide an added margin of safety, start the swing with the club face slightly open and*

*finish with the palm of the left hand down-
ward to insure that the face remains open during the entire swing.*

When I began to make a close study of my sand
shots I noticed that whenever the ball lay close to the
front bank of the trap and required loft quickly I almost invariably got the ball out nicely. But when the
ball lay near the center of the rear of the trap, and thus
called for no immediate loft, I tended to carelessness
and was more prone to leave the ball in the trap or
knock it all the way over the green. With this in mind,
I started the practice of building a sort of imaginary
mound a foot or two in front of my ball so as to make
myself strive for quick height whether it was actually
needed or not. I found this a great help. Try it if you
have trouble in sand traps.

Once the basic method of simple escape from the
sand is firmly established, it becomes possible to work
on getting close to the hole from this position. This
involves adjustments either in the distance behind the
ball that your clubhead strikes the sand, or in the
power of your swing, or in a combination of the two.
With nearly all good sand players it is a combination of
the two adjustments, with emphasis on the latter. The
power of the swing should range from three-quarter

power down to less than half. The distance you hit behind the ball should remain fairly constant at about two inches. Getting the ball close to the hole then becomes a matter of touch, just as a chip shot or putt is a matter of touch, or, as Ben Hogan called it, "muscle memory."

Texture and depth of sand are the factors that control distance, assuming equal swing power and space between club face and ball at the bottom of the swing. Sand that is wet, coarse or shallow will make for distance, separately and in combination. Sand that is deep and powdery is the toughest to get out of. It calls for a full-explosion shot with a firm follow-through. Look for sand newly placed in traps and not yet packed down to be of the latter type. Depth of sand can be gauged as you dig in to get a firm stance.

For golfers with a long standing fear of sand traps, or who find themselves in the throes of a temporary sand slump, I prescribe a session of thirty minutes or so in a practice trap. Before trying to hit the first ball out of the trap, take practice swings until you are able consistently to take sand divots of uniform size about a half to three-quarters inch deep and about six inches long, following through to a full finish on each swing. Then drop a ball in the sand and try an actual shot with the same swing. Repeat this pattern half a dozen times or so. This method will work for you.

Shots from bad lies in sand traps call for a considerably different technique than shots from normal lies.

When a golf ball plops into a sand trap and stays where it hits, it generally produces what is called the "fried-egg lie." Usually the ball will be about half buried and will be ringed by a slight depression some six

SAND TRAP

"FRIED EGG LIE"

inches across. It is not an easy shot to play. Getting it out calls for a strong downward blow with the club striking the sand about two inches behind the ball. To accentuate the downward, chopping character of the blow, position the ball about on a line with the right heel. Little follow-through can be expected on this shot since the clubhead must be driven into the sand to a depth of two or three inches to dig the ball out, but try for as much follow-through as your strength will permit.

196

On this shot there will be little underspin, so allow for some roll.

If the ball is buried deep in the sand, close your club face slightly. This will give you a more pronounced digging angle. This shot also demands a full swing because all or nearly all of your power will be needed to bring the ball upward and out on to the green.

On this type of shot my method is to fix my eyes on the spot where I mean for my clubhead to enter the sand, rather than on the ball. This holds true in all cases where the principal objective is simply escaping from the trap. On shots from normal or near-normal lies where there is a better chance of gauging the distance and getting near the hole I fix my eye on the ball itself. There are, however, some good sand players who, as the phrase goes, look at the sand instead of the ball; but they are in the minority.

When the ball buries itself extremely deep in heavy sand it is often more effective to use a pitching wedge or a nine-iron to get it out, for the reason that the sharper leading edge of the club will make it easier to get deeper into the sand. We have seen that the flange on the wedge will cause the club to bounce forward and through the sand, which is highly undesirable when the objective is to dig as deep into the sand as possible.

Shots from uphill lies in sand traps call for a change in stance, putting most of the weight on the right foot so that the body position conforms to the contour of the slope on which the ball rests. The ball should be positioned about on a line with the right toe so that the clubhead will enter the sand at the end of its downward arc. It will do no harm if the sand is hit slightly after the upward arc is begun. Swing to the uphill lie, the sand through which the clubhead must pass will be deeper as the clubhead moves toward and past the ball. Hence your aim should be adjusted to hit slightly closer to the ball than would be the case from a flat lie.

When the ball is near-buried in an upslope and the bunker overhangs, it will be helpful to take the club back slightly outside the line so as to come into the ball from outside in. This is the same type of stroke that produces a slice or fade on a normal shot. This cutting action will make it easier for the clubhead to get through the sand and will help in getting immediate loft to clear the overhanging bunker.

For downhill lies in sand traps the adjustments called for are the reverse of those used from uphill lies:

weight principally on left foot, ball positioned about on line with the right heel, and sand entered with club-head about a half inch further back on the ball than would be the case with a flat lie.

On very short sand trap shots, where the ball lies very close to the edge of the green and the pin is spotted near the trap, the technique indicated is the same as for a normal sand shot, except that the follow-through should be shortened. In this situation virtually any movement of the sand will send the ball into the green and the shortened follow-through will cut down on distance. This is not to say that you should just stick the clubhead into the sand behind the ball with no follow-through at all. There should be a definite follow-through, but the clubhead should go past the ball only about three feet.

The chip shot from the sand trap is at times the wisest shot to choose, but it is always attended with a certain amount of danger. The first essential condition for this shot is a clean lie in the trap with no sand hiding any part of the back of the ball. And it should be tried only when there is no high bank to clear at the front of the trap.

The proper technique calls for the weight mostly on the left foot and the ball positioned slightly nearer the right foot than would be the case with a chip from the grass. The player must be absolutely certain that the ball is struck first, since if any sand is hit behind the ball the clubhead will tend to hang in the sand and the result will be spoiled. The downswing on this shot is down and through the ball as with any chip shot. The shot should be tried only when there is room between the front edge of the green and the pin to permit a fairly sizable amount of roll, say thirty feet or more. The shot does not lend itself to quick stopping.

Keep in mind that this chip from the sand is a delicate shot requiring steady nerves and a confident stroke. When there is doubt as to the wisdom of trying the shot, the doubt should almost always be resolved in favor of the safer explosion shot.

Use of the putter from the sand has a definite place in golf. It can at times be the safest shot of all. The first requirement for this shot, as with the chip, is a clean lie in the trap. Another essential condition is a smooth ascent from the trap and no overhanging lip. A ball solidly struck with the putter will climb up most any bank of less than ninety degree incline, provided the ball is rolling along the top of the sand and not lofted into the bank. The utmost care must be exercised to insure that the ball is struck solidly in the center. Hit too low, the ball may be lofted and will hit and stop in soft sand. If the ball is hit on top it will be mashed down in the sand to start with, and will roll only a few feet. In wet, hard or shallow sand, the putt is usually fairly safe. In sand that is soft and deep, this shot is dangerous.

A shot from a sand trap that is not a full shot, yet requires a considerable carry, is about as tough a shot as there is in golf. The explosion shot executed properly will hardly carry more than thirty yards, and when greater carry is needed, and the lie is not a good one, it will be necessary to hit the ball and the sand almost together. This becomes very difficult any time the ball is even slightly embedded in the trap. The best method here is to close the face of the wedge slightly and try to catch the ball and sand at the same time. When the lie is a clean one, the ball can be hit first and the distance can be gauged with a fair degree of accuracy.

When maximum distance is required from a sand trap, everything will depend on the lie and the loft needed to get the ball out of the trap and on its way. With a clean lie and no high bank in front, the shot can be played in much the same way as a shot from the fairway. A prime consideration is to dig the feet far enough down into the sand to insure as firm a footing as possible. The feet are apt to shift position in the sand, with dire consequences, any time a full body turn is taken. This can be at least partially offset by swinging mostly with the arms and shoulders, immobilizing the body as much as possible.

With a fairly poor lie in a sand trap and the situation calling urgently for distance, the best shot may be a deliberate half-topped shot with a medium iron. Obviously this shot should be attempted only when immediate loft is not a consideration. This is a tough shot to make, and should only be tried when desperate measures are called for. Further, if the shot is successful the ball is apt to be cut to the cover and rendered useless for further play.

There are rare occasions when a wood club (three-wood or four-wood) should be used from a sand trap to get needed distance. The lie must, of course, be exceptionally good, and no obstacles to the front. To make the shot, get as firm a footing as the sand will permit. As a safety measure, open the club face slightly and allow for a slice on the shot. This adjustment will permit the sole of the club to strike the sand first on any swing that causes the clubhead to hit slightly behind the ball, and the clubhead will tend to bounce forward into the ball. Here again the shot is a delicate one, and probably should be tried only by the better golfers.

One more thing about sand traps: They can be extremely treacherous, and especially so in medal play. The case of Sam Snead in the 1955 Masters Tournament provides a vivid illustration of the point.

Snead came to the 13th hole in the first round of this tournament three under par and playing beautifully. His second shot on this 13th hole, which is a fairly short but highly dangerous par-five, carried into a new trap at the left side of the green and buried itself in the soft sand at the back of the trap. To try to knock the ball out toward the hole, Snead had to take a chance of jamming the ball further down in the sand, and that is what he did on his first try. When he finally dislodged the ball and got out he was on in six and two-putted for an eight on the hole. So there he was back to even par, and the hole that did it to him was one on which he could expect a birdie about 50 per cent of the time. A lot of people at the tournament said Sam never got over that tough break, and that it cost him the tournament. (I won it, incidentally.)

What Snead might have done in this situation—

and what he would have done if foresight were as good as hindsight—would have been to concentrate solely on dislodging the ball on the first stroke from the sand. He could have done this by playing the ball toward the side of the green rather than toward the pin. But, being a powerful man and a very good sand player, he elected to take a chance that worked out badly.

The moral being that if it is sometimes wise for Sam Snead to be very cautious with buried lies in sand traps, it will sometimes be wise for all of us to be.

○ ○ ○ ○ ○ ○ ○ ○ ○ ○ ○ ○ ○ ○ 14

Uneven Lies

THE CHIEF THING to remember about uneven lies—by which is meant lies in which one foot is higher than the other or in which the ball is on a different level than the feet—is that a definite alteration in your swinging pattern must be made.

Take first a downhill lie: Since the ground behind the ball is higher than that on which the ball sits, you would be most foolish to try to hit the shot with your normal ball placement and swing. If you did, you would certainly hit the ground behind the ball—quite possibly so far behind it that the club would bounce right over the top of the ball.

One thing that must be done, then, is to stand so that the bottom of the arc of your swing will be reached at the ball. This simply calls for placing the ball nearer your right foot. How much nearer would

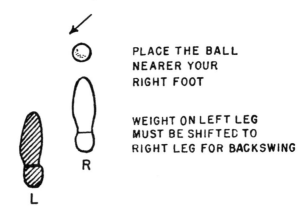

PLACE THE BALL
NEARER YOUR
RIGHT FOOT

WEIGHT ON LEFT LEG
MUST BE SHIFTED TO
RIGHT LEG FOR BACKSWING

DOWNHILL LIE

depend on the grade of the incline on which the ball lies. Without going into degrees and such, I would say that the average downhill lie calls for placing the ball about even with the right heel.

That done, you should give consideration to the fact that a little extra effort will be needed to get the weight over to your right leg for the backswing, and there will be a tendency to shift too much and too quickly to the left leg for the downswing. This would result in your getting your body ahead of your hands on the downswing, which would mean a pushed shot.

Since your hitting action is going to have to be different from your normal pattern, it will be wise to take a couple of practice swings before hitting this type of shot. Do this to fit your swing to the contour of the ground.

Now as to the choice of a club for a shot from a downhill lie: First I would eliminate as possibilities on this type of shot the two-wood and the one-iron. If the lie is downhill to any appreciable extent, neither of these clubs have enough loft to get the ball more than barely airborne. Assuming a slope of fifteen degrees and a club loft of fifteen degrees, one offsets the other. If you think a shot from a downhill lie is, say, of five-iron distance, take your five-iron—but remember that the ball is bound to come out in a low trajectory and that if you hit the shot with all your power you will get a little more distance than you would on the same shot from a level lie. I do not, however, recommend that you hit the shot with full power. Choke down on the grip and hit well within your maximum power, because you are in a relatively strange situation calling for caution.

On the follow-through, make your clubhead follow the contour of the hill for about a foot past the ball. This will allow time for the ball to roll up the face of the club and insure some height, and will help prevent your getting your body in ahead of the hands and clubhead.

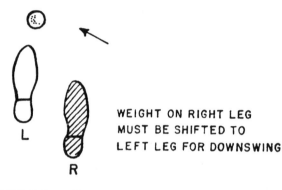

WEIGHT ON RIGHT LEG
MUST BE SHIFTED TO
LEFT LEG FOR DOWNSWING

L

R

UPHILL LIE

Now uphill lies: This shot is in nearly all respects opposite from the shot from the downhill lie. The bottom of your swing arc will be reached at a later point than normally, hence you should position the ball at address farther forward than you would on a normal lie. For most uphill lies, about even with the left toe should do.

The weight shifting problem is quite simply reversed. With your left foot higher than your right, it will be natural and easy to transfer the weight to the right leg on the backswing. But a small amount of extra effort will be needed to shift it back over to the left leg for the downswing. Take a couple of practice swings to accustom yourself to the situation you are in. If your body stays behind your hands you are virtually certain to pull the shot hard to the left.

For uphill lies, as for downhill lies, I favor a swing well within your maximum power, with the club gripped about an inch lower on the shaft than normal. For this reason, plus the fact that the up-slope will add to the normal loft of your club in proportion to the grade of the slope, you should take at least one bigger club than the distance itself would call for. Frequently two clubs more will be the proper answer.

As on downhill lies, let the clubhead follow the contour of the ground for a foot or more past the ball. To be able to do so requires a proper shifting of the weight, so that if you consciously determine to do this you will be helped in getting your weight back over to the left leg on the downswing. Thus eliminating the flat-footed hit that is common from uphill lies.

On shots where the ball is above the feet, your swing will of necessity be a flat one. Even to make contact between the clubhead and the ball you will have to swing in a definite inside-to-outside pattern. I think you will readily see the physical near-impossibility of cutting across a shot in this situation. Further, the follow-through will naturally be in a sort of circular pattern.

All these factors tend to produce a hook or pull, or a combination of the two. The simplest solution here is simply to allow for a considerable left draw and go ahead and hit the shot. If the shot situation does not allow room to play for this hook-pull, open the club face some and make the shot with the hands staying ahead of the clubhead.

As on all uneven lies, remember that you are having to use an altered swing, so avail yourself of two or three practice swings under comparable conditions. Get the new swing pattern firmly fixed in your mind before making the shot.

The other type of sidehill lie is the one where the ball lies below the feet. Naturally this calls for an upright swing. You will have to stand closer to the ball, with reference to its distance from your feet, in order to hit it—although, of course, the distance between the ball and the hands remains constant.

The big danger here is that as you make your downswing you are apt to be pulled forward by the centrifugal force that emanates from your swing, causing you to hit the ball in the neck of the club, and possibly to shank it. You must set your weight solidly on your heels at the outset of the stroke, and consciously resist this forward pull. The prescribed practice swings will be helpful in this respect.

The natural tendency is to slice or push the ball on these shots where the ball is below the feet. This tendency will be minimized, however, if you can manage to keep your weight planted solidly on your heels throughout the swing.

A specialized type of action is called for when you are standing on level ground with the ball well below the feet, as might happen if the shot was from the bottom of a narrow parallel ditch. Here the secret is to immobilize the body as completely as possible and make the shot with only the arms and shoulders in action.

With reference to lies, always remember that when the ball is imbedded in wet grass, or in the soft type of grass usually found on Eastern courses, you are apt to get some extra distance by virtue of the fact that a layer of grass will be between the club face and the ball at contact. This type of lie produces the "sailing" shot, with very little underspin. To get better control, position the ball a little further forward and use a sweeping kind of a stroke. In the South, the grass and turf are usually hard and dry, making it virtually impossible to hit too much of a descending blow on the ball.

Where the ground is soft or sandy, you must be careful to keep your feet from shifting position during the swing. To do this, dig the feet in a little in taking your stance and then swing more flat-footed than normal.

This is something that Ben Hogan evidentally neglected to do on the 18th hole in his playoff with Jack Fleck for the 1955 National Open. The 18th hole there at the Lakeside Club in San Francisco was one of several on the course that had new tees which were soft and sandy. On his tee shot, Hogan's feet moved just enough to cause him to lose control. The result was a big hook into very deep rough, from which he was unable to recover. Of course, he probably would have lost anyway, being a stroke down with one hole left to play, but that bad tee shot cost him whatever chance he had.

Around, Over, Under

I T HARDLY NEEDS to be argued that the ability to hook or slice a golf ball deliberately when the situation calls for it, is a valuable asset to a golfer. So let's proceed to the matter of how to do it, beginning with the slice.

A golf ball curves to the right for a right-handed player for the one essential reason that a left-to-right spin is imparted to it while the clubhead is in contact with the ball. This type of spin may be imparted in two ways:

1. *The clubhead may be drawn across the ball from right to left on the downswing.*
2. *The clubface may be slanted to the right (open) at impact.*

Either one of these methods can be used to produce a shot that follows a left-to-right path of flight, and the two can be used in combination so that each will augment the other.

The simplest method of causing the ball to follow a left-to-right pattern of flight is to set the clubhead back of the ball square to the objective in the normal way, slant the club face open a few degrees, grip the club with the face of it still open, and swing as for a straight ball. Meeting the ball with the club face still open tends to produce a shot that has a slight left-to-right curve on it, due to the spin on the ball produced by the open club face. This shot is of some value in sending the ball around an obstacle.

The next simplest way to slice is by adjusting the grip. Bring the knuckles of the left hand back under the shaft and fold the right hand over the top of the shaft. A wide slice figures to result if the V formed by the thumb and first finger of the left hand points to the right shoulder, and that V on the right hand points toward the left shoulder. (With the normal grip, the two Vs will be just about parallel and pointing slightly to the right of the chin.) This slice grip will cause the club face to sort of flip open as the clubhead comes into the ball. This result figures to be a shot that starts off fairly straight but starts following a left-to-right pattern a few yards after leaving the clubface.

The slice shot that is generally the most effective in getting around obstacles is the one that travels several yards in a straight line after leaving the club face, and then curves rather abruptly to the right. This action is the one produced by drawing the club face across the ball from right to left in the latter stages of the downswing. The best method for bringing this about is to start the clubhead back from the ball outside the line. Having done so, and assuming no offsetting adjustments during the course of the swing, the clubhead will come back into the ball from the outside in—or across the ball. With this type of stroke, the forward power of the swing will send the ball out in a generally straight line until the left-to-right spin, caused by the clubhead's slicing across the ball, takes effect.

Here is a simple way of achieving the proper start on the backswing for a deliberate slice: After lining up in the normal way to the shot, pick out sqme small object that catches the eye about a foot back of the ball and about two inches to the right of the ball. A particular blade of grass will do. Then set it in your mind that the clubhead must pass over the top of that small object on the backswing.

Now for a way of trying to insure that nothing happens during the course of the swing to offset the cut-across pattern you have set up by taking the club-head back outside the line: Determine to pattern your swing so that at the end of the follow-through the palm of your left hand will be down and roughly parallel with the ground—or, if you prefer to think of it another way—that the back of your left hand will be up. This action will keep the hands from rolling over, which is, naturally, a part of the hooking action.

Of itself, the stance will have nothing to do with whether the shot slices, but an open stance makes it easier to produce a slicing swing.

The open stance simply calls for advancing the right foot about six inches closer to the intended line of flight than the left. The effect will be to move the left hip out of the way of the arms so that the clubhead may be easily brought across the ball, and to place the right hip *in* the way so that the arms will have to go out and around it and produce an outside-in swing.

216

It is clear, I think, that the sliced ball can result from any of a number of factors, or from any combination of these factors, provided there is no offsetting action in the rest of the swing. An example of such offsetting action would occur if the hands were permitted to roll over as the clubhead came into the ball. That is to say that a player might adjust his grip for a slice, take the club away from the ball outside the line, and try to cut across the ball, but if the hands rolled over quickly just before impact, the shot would tend to go straight, or even hook. (There are, indeed, many players who use some part of the slicing method in the early stages of the swing to offset a natural tendency to hook.)

How much of a slice can an ordinary player expect to put on a given shot? This is a question that naturally enters the picture here. There are many factors to be considered in this connection, the chief one being the type of swing the player naturally has. The golfer who tends to slice normally can, by consciously applying one or more of the slicing techniques, bring about a very wide curve to the right. The natural hooker will have more trouble, but should be able to call forth a slice at any time by concentrating on drawing the club face across the ball. If the hook will take note of the finish of his normal swing, he will almost certainly find that the position of his hands will be palm of right hand facing down, and palm of left hand up; showing that his hands have rolled over during the swing. So, in virtually all cases, the natural hooker who needs a slice should put his main concentration on finishing the swing with left palm down and right palm up.

The loft of the club has much to do with the amount of slice that can be produced. The lesser the loft the greater the ease with which the ball may be sliced, and the greater the slice that can be put on it. Thus, if a deliberate slice is called for, take a club with as little loft as is practicable. The reasoning here is that the more lofted clubs put more underspin on the ball, and what we are looking for to produce the slice is sidespin (left to right). Some better players even use a putter when an extreme slice is needed from distances of 100 to 150 yards. If you try this shot, however, be sure that your putter has a strong shaft, and that you open the club face wide enough to get some loft on the ball.

Making aiming adjustments for slicing around obstacles is a matter of individual judgment. A little practice should show a golfer how much he can expect to

slice a ball when he needs to. He should remember
that a wind blowing into him will make slicing easy,
and that a following wind will straighten the ball out.

THE HOOK

The methods to use in causing the ball to hook
are in all respects opposite to those used in producing
the slice. The hook is simply the result of a right-to-
left spin put on the ball while the clubhead is in contact with the ball.

The simplest and easiest method of bringing
about a right-to-left pattern of flight for a shot is to
turn the club face in, grip the club with the face thus
closed, and swing as for a straight ball. This method
will bring about some right-to-left curve, with the ball
taking off immediately to the left.

A hook may also be brought about by an adjustment of the grip that puts the right hand more under
the shaft and the left hand more on top of the shaft
(the exact opposite of the slice grip). As a check, see
that the V's formed by the thumb and first finger of
each hand point toward the right hip. The first three
knuckles of the left hand should be visible looking
straight down the shaft.

The sweeping right-to-left curve that starts fairly straight is produced by an inside-out swing that brings the clubhead into the ball by a path opposite to that of the cut-across swing. This action, if pronounced, will start the ball out a little to the right before the hook takes effect.

This inside-out swing can be best achieved by taking the clubhead away from the ball slightly inside the line and rolling the hands as the clubhead comes into the ball. To insure that the hands roll over during the swing, simply pattern the stroke so that at the finish the palm of the right hand will be down and the palm of the left hand up.

The widest hooks can be achieved with clubs of medium depth. The four-wood and the four-iron are apt to be the clubs with which you can produce the biggest hook. With the straighter faced clubs, like the driver and the two-iron, there is a danger of not getting the ball sufficiently high to get a wide hook, since the hook swing brings the clubhead into the ball with the face closed. The deeper clubs tend to produce too much underspin to permit a wide and continuing hook.

The degree to which a ball can be hooked depends largely on the natural swing tendencies of the individual player. Most experts can hook in about the same degree that they can slice. A golfer who naturally slices will have trouble producing a hook, but will generally be able to do so if he concentrates on a finish that sees the palm of the right hand down and the palm of the left hand up.

Implicit in these instructions for slicing and hooking are some pointers for those players who are continually trying to *keep from* doing either. The golfer who is always fighting a hook could hardly do better than to practice a finish with the right palm facing up. In this way he can do much to eliminate the hand roll that is the cause of most troublesome hooks. The natural slicer should reverse the pattern.

THE LOW SHOT

To produce a low-flying shot of the type often needed to keep the ball under some tree limbs or other obstacle, the ball must be hit with a downward blow and the club face should be slightly closed. Also, the ball must be struck definitely ahead of the turf. This type of swing is made easier by positioning the ball nearer the right foot. If a very low shot is required, position the ball back about even with the right toe.

The ball is positioned well to the right of center for a low shot in order to insure that the ball will be struck before the downswing is completed, and while the hands are slightly ahead of the clubhead. It may be easily seen, I think, that a shot of normal height would result if the ball were hit just at the end of the downswing with the hands about even with the club-head.

THE HIGH SHOT

To hit a deliberately high shot in order to clear some intervening obstacle the method is, naturally enough, the opposite of that used for a low shot. Ball positioning is the chief factor. The ball should be positioned so that it can be hit either at the very end of the downswing or at the beginning of the upswing. If much height is needed, the ball at address should be about even with the left toe. On all shots where height is a factor, the club face should be left slightly open at address.

Care must be taken when attempting a high shot to see that the hands do not roll over as the clubhead comes into the ball, closing the club face. The recommended method here is the same as for the slice swing—finish with the left palm facing down.

SUMMARY

Having acquired some knowledge of the methods for going around, under, and over obstacles, some further knowledge will be needed as to when to apply these methods. That is to say that they should not be overused. At times you will be in positions where the slice or hook or the low shot or high shot offers the only possible chance, or offers the best chance. At other times the better method may be to sacrifice a shot in order that the next shot will be a clear one. The low shot, in particular, is a dangerous one for the average player, with little margin for error offered between the shot that rises too quickly and the one that doesn't rise at all. The high shot is, generally speaking, easier, and the slice and hook, once mastered, can almost always be counted on.

All players should be on guard, however, against attempting the impossible or the near-impossible. This is, of course, especially true in medal play, where a very bad hole can virtually eliminate all chance of victory. In match play, where only one hole can be lost at a time, bigger chances can be taken.

Index